Saying Goodbye

Saying Goodbye

Resources for funerals, scattering ashes and remembering

Ruth Burgess

wild goose
publications

www.**ionabooks**.com

First published 2013 by
Wild Goose Publications, Fourth Floor, Savoy House,
140 Sauchiehall Street, Glasgow G2 3DH, UK,
the publishing division of the Iona Community.
Scottish Charity No. SC003794. Limited Company Reg. No. SC096243.

ISBN 978-1-84952-274-8

Cover photograph © Ewing Wallace

The publishers gratefully acknowledge the support of the Drummond Trust,
3 Pitt Terrace, Stirling FK8 2EY in producing this book.

Overseas distribution
Australia: Willow Connection Pty Ltd, Unit 4A, 3–9 Kenneth Road, Manly Vale, NSW 2093
New Zealand: Pleroma, Higginson Street, Otane 4170, Central Hawkes Bay
Canada: Bayard Distribution, 10 Lower Spadina Ave., Suite 400, Toronto, Ontario M5V 2Z

Printed by Bell & Bain, Thornliebank, Glasgow

Contents

Contents in detail

Key to symbols	
✟	Prayer
⚕	Liturgy
(((○)))	Responsive prayer
♫	Song
▤	Letter
✪	Reflective prayer
♥	Meditation
⊞	Reflection
✭	Poem
⛲	Creed
ᕲ	Reading
⛓	Practical

Key to symbols	
✝	Prayer
𝒮	Liturgy
(((◉)))	Responsive prayer
♫	Song
📧	Letter
✿	Reflective prayer
♥	Meditation
▦	Reflection
✿	Poem
⛵	Creed
𝒸	Reading
🚲	Practical

Life goes on - words for the journey   187

Life without end   193

Appendix   197

Key to symbols

Symbol	Meaning
✝	Prayer
⌇	Liturgy
((◉))	Responsive prayer
♫	Song
🗎	Letter
✿	Reflective prayer
♥	Meditation
⊞	Reflection
✿	Poem
⛏	Creed
ᕙ	Reading
᪥	Practical

For Lynda,
who kept on asking

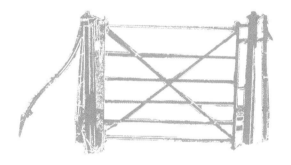

Introduction

Saying Goodbye is a resource book for anyone who is planning a funeral. You may be a family member or friend of someone who has died. You may be planning your own funeral. You may arrange and conduct funerals professionally.

This is a book full of words and ideas for those looking for ways of celebrating a person's life which are personal and honest.

Not everyone attending a funeral will have a conventional religious faith. There are resources in this book that do not assume a faith commitment, as well as resources that reflect Christian belief.

Whilst a number of complete liturgies are included, most of the material in this book consists of the stuff that liturgies are made of: responses, readings, rituals, actions, biblical reflections, poems, songs and prayers.

There is a section on the involvement of children in funeral services. And there are words that could be used when scattering or burying ashes.

At the back of the book there is an Appendix with a section on planning an order of service for a funeral, some ideas for a day conference on funerals, lists of helpful websites and books, and some empty pages for you to collect any other ideas or readings that you come across and want to remember.

I am grateful to all the contributors to this book for their rich and varied material and for their helpful and supportive correspondence. The quality of contributors' writing is a delight. This book grew out of a larger book, and a volume containing resources for baptisms, naming ceremonies, civil partnerships and marriages will follow.

Thanks are due to the Wild Goose Publications team: Sandra Kramer, Jane Darroch Riley, Alex O'Neill and Susie Hay. A huge thank you to Neil Paynter for his legendary attention to detail and for his awareness of what works and what 'sings'. Thanks to Ewing Wallace for photography. Thank you, too, to Elizabeth Wild, Ruth Harvey, Pat Welburn, John and Molly Harvey, Lynda Wright, Sally Foster-Fulton and Brid Fitzpatrick for wise advice.

One of the contributors to this book told me: 'I am passionate about people having a good funeral.' I share this passion. I hope this book further resources us to lovingly and honestly tell people's stories and to say goodbye.

When it is my time to go
I want you to tell my story as it was,
to give God thanks,
and to throw my ashes to the elements –
to the fire,
to the wind,
to the earth,
to the sea –
and then go
and have tea.

If I change my mind (and I might)
and decide to be buried
I'll let you know.

Enough for now to know that
coming and going
we are loved
and called to be loving,
and we belong to God.

Ruth Burgess, spring 2013

Last months and days

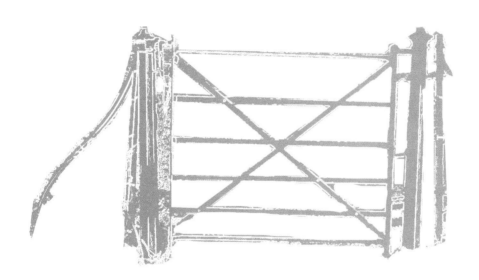

Notice to quit

There comes a day when it becomes reality
that the long, blessed holiday will end.

There comes a letter saying, yes, there is some leeway,
but the ferry is arranged.

Expect to pay before you reach the jetty.
That is the way these leavings go.

The day came yesterday,
the letter just a line or so

offering an appointment –
hardly a subtle code.

Such a rich present to have had
from a good friend,

more sunsets still to see
before it ends.

Roddy Cowie

Special pleading

Once more
to see a snowdrop
to smell the sea
once more
once more
to hold the child
to be a wordsmith
once more
once more
to dance a reel
dive into a pool
once more
once more
once more
once more, O Lord.
once more.

Kate McIlhagga

The time that's left

God bless to me the time that's left:
to hold the child,
to see another spring,
to tidy my room,
to forgive and forget,
to reach out and befriend,
to live my life in peace and joy.
God bless to me
eternity.

Kate McIlhagga

Dementia (observed)

I went with her to the consultant;
his brutality shocked me:
'You have dementia. It will get worse,
then you will die.'
I came away in disbelief.
In vain I'd tried suggesting
it might be loneliness
exacerbating memory loss.

At first it was the computer,
my husband patiently explaining it to her,
again and then again.
Next the TV became complex,
even switching it on and off.

Assessments led to agency care,
fiercely resisted, angry storms
and then the alcohol.
Sometimes manic scenes
alternating with frightened
childhood tears.

Gradually the world was shrinking:
the dog was wonderful,
slowing down beside her,
the only one she'd really
need to speak to.
Neighbours were all enemies.
They were multiplied, watching, invading,
harming the beloved pets.

One summer she could still admire
the flowers and vegetables,
once-expert gardener
remembering how to treat the weeds.
Then next year, nothing.

'What should I do?'
Which sock to wear or shoe?
Panicked repetitions of time and date,
the door key lost
and unaware of an unlocked house.
And yet the moods were softening,
smiles now and then,
and even appreciating the weekly outing,
something inside transforming
as connections past and present snapped.

What triggered the next step down I do not know.
Long wanderings
alarming carers,
decisions made for full-time care.
I never thought she would accept it,
but now detachment, even from the dog,
confused like her in new surroundings.

'No,' I say, 'she wasn't married.
She was a lecturer, training teachers,
preacher in her church, fundraiser.'
This illness of the brain,
a strange, prolonged way of dying.
A dark hole with dangerous suction.

I pray the little glimpses of the light
will fill the space
until the Easter hope is realised.

Liz Gregory-Smith

A prayer for Peggy

God remembers you:
your name and your story,
today
and every day;

in the darkness before morning
you are not alone;

in the questions without answers
you are not unheard.

Whatever happens to you,
you will always be yourself.

God is on your road;
God walks with you
all the smiles
and tears of your journey.

Today and every day,
God remembers you
with love.

Ruth Burgess

Saying goodbye

What words to use
to say goodbye?
Ravel piano music
threads through
our conversation
as I struggle to find the words.

An opportunity arises,
enables me to express
regret at the short time
of acquaintance.
Do you sense what I mean?

The moment passes,
more talk; I leave;
in silence.
We share a hug
full of love
in saying goodbye.

Katherine Rennie

Last Supper

He seemed thinner, smaller, than he had
during my childhood; an old man, huddled
in his chair, which, as children, we relinquished
unwillingly every day on his return from work.
I sat in mother's place: the seat she vacated
more than years 20 before – too many packets
of Players with the jaunty sailor on the front –
no dire warnings then that smoking could
damage your health, or may cause death.

Munching our batter fritters by the fire –
only dad could make them taste like this,
due no doubt to an apprenticeship forged
in deep-fried fat during the 1930s when
his horse-drawn fish and chip cart brought

'bawbee sustenance' to a community
starved by the Depression's deprivations –
I enquired 'Fancy a run up the moor after supper?'
His faded blue eyes lit up and he nodded.

Muffled in his worn-out jacket and faded flat cap,
I drove him up Clayport Bank; we parked atop
the hill and watched the sunset over Cheviot
turn Whittingham Vale to glorious gold.
'The grandest view in the world,' he said.
Metaphorically I punched the air in delight
at this admission; my Northumbrian triumph
was short-lived. 'Outside Scotland, that is,'
he added, his eyes a-twinkle, Scot to the last.

Next Friday I arrived at teatime to find
he wasn't there; at the infirmary
I picked up his few possessions –
a hearing aid still whistling in the box.
I drove to Corby's Crags and wound
the window down to watch the sunset.
Inhaling temperate evening air,
I thought I caught a whiff
of batter fritters.

Carol Dixon

Walking along the shore (thoughts of Helen)

I walk on the shore,
black stones shift beneath my feet.
You are not walking now.

I walk along the shore,
waves come and go,
time comes and goes;
shores mark a beginning or an ending.
You are at a shore
where days end and expanse waits.
'At the end, there is a beginning.'

I pick up fossils, to name or date;
they are older than you or me;
older than flesh and blood;
they have seen people come
and people go.

The wind chases the water,
tousles my hair,
the air fresh and disturbing.
Your breath struggles,
comes and goes.

Birds call – loud, raucous, informative.
Your music called, sensitive and probing,
opening minds and closed days.
You gave the gift of calling to many,
calls which will not go away.

A TB clinic stands grey on the hill;
patients used to lie outside in fresh-air beds.
You lie in your hospice bed,
sharing times with your daughter.

The sun glows gold,
throwing its colour
across the western sky;
its farewell gleam on the stony shore
throwing black rocks into relief,
highlighting small black waterbirds.

The day is ending,
defined by this glorious,
golden light.

Judy Dinnen

Saying goodbye to Jean

Dear friend, lying with no more gifts to give:
Dear seed, you withered long before you fell into the ground.

Why did you will yourself to reach the time
when there was nothing left but bones lit up with pain?

What harvest could there be from such a harrowing?
A stone forces itself into my mind, with this inscription:

Find a way of saying death is acceptable.
Let it be there when I come to the river.

I have no wish to fight my way along its banks:
Let me relax my will, and dive.

Roddy Cowie

Dying and death

Remember me in my dying

Lord of all life,
when others died I thought of death as part of nature:
a rose flourishing, bestowing fragrance, and returning to earth.
Now that death draws nearer me
it is not fear – but wonder that fills me,
when I think of the speck I was in the womb
and what I tried to accomplish over the years.
For death itself I trust Jesus's promises;
but dying may be hard to bear,
possibly in unremitting pain with the body out of control,
a stranger to the mind.

Lord of all life, remember me in my dying;
remember us all in our dying.

Ian M. Fraser

Prayers with those who are dying

This morning my husband, David, who is a minister, visited a man in a hospice. The man was concerned for those of his family who have supported him, and grateful to the hospital and hospice. He was coming to terms with the short time he had to live, and needed to engage in the task of dying and preparing others for his death …

Living God, behind us, before us, beyond us
we so greatly value this time …

The struggle for peace; the gift of acceptance,
and the special task that falls to us
as we prepare those around us
for what lies ahead.

For the things we still need to say, give space
and help us to offload
every loose end that is still beyond us.

Complete for us
the forgiveness we begin.

Help us to know that, with you, our best is enough.

Above all, give comfort to those who have cared,
who have been there when we needed them.
With you there is no need to hide
or water down
what friends are sad to hear.

God, give us the hope that does not rely on our own strength.

Zam Walker and David Coleman

Dysfunctional fractions

I don't like math very much, and have never been good at it either. I can use percentages to figure out a tip or a sale price, but that's about it. Math just doesn't do it for me – and fractions used to drive me crazy! I never did care why Suzie got 1/4 and Johnny got 1/4 but Mary got 1/2 of the dessert.

However, recently I've been thinking about fractions very differently. In my work as a chaplain, I met a teenage father who said 'his heart is broken into pieces' due to his child's medical condition and imminent death. He explained that his family and the child's mother's family are divided over what should be done at the time of death. They are split as to whether or not their child should be cremated or buried. Also, due to the nature of the family divisions, each 24-hour period is split in half. The mother may visit for 12 hours and the father may visit for 12 hours, but they may not overlap.

He said he preferred that their child be cremated, so that the mother can bury half of the ashes and he can keep half of the ashes with him at all times. I wrote down this information, as standard documentation of parental desires, but after I wrote it I stared down at my notes. 'Father prefers cremation and requests he receive 1/2 of ashes and requests mother receive 1/2 of ashes.'

While this actually made perfect sense emotionally after listening to him, it made no sense to see 1/2 and 1/2 written about a child. I wondered 'which half will go with which parent?'; and 'do you tell other family members and generations that the site they are visiting only contains half of their loved one?' …

I cannot imagine having a fraction of ashes from anyone I love, and I witnessed his pain multiplied by the thought of his only having 1/2 of his child's remains. His family is in pieces. His heart is in pieces. He cannot help his child. He cannot put his family back together. He can only see his child during 1/2 of the day. Everything about his life is divided into fractions.

As I continued to listen to his pain through his tears, I prayed for God to make something – anything – whole again for this man. And I gave thanks to God that this child would soon be whole again. This child will no longer be sick or in pain or the centre of custody battles. This child will know the unconditional love of Christ, who welcomes all children to a home that is far from broken. For this child, wholeness, restoration and peace will come by leaving the divisions of this world behind. For this child, being in heaven equals being whole.

I don't know what wholeness will look like for this father or mother, but I pray God picks up the pieces and puts each one back in its place until their hearts and souls are whole again.

A. A. Masters

It's time to go

It's time to go.
It's OK to go.
We're here.
We love you.

It's been a fight for you.
We've watched you struggle,
watched your body dying,
seen you in sadness and pain.

It's hard.
This saying goodbye.
You love us.
We love you.
You don't want to go.

And we don't want you to go
but we know that you need to.
Your time here is over,
your job is done.

There's a time for fighting.
You've always been a fighter.
You're not going to change now.
We know that.
We know you.

But we need to tell you
that we're here
beside you,
and we're OK,
we'll miss you but we'll manage,
and we'll be here,
loving you
when you let go.

Ruth Burgess

The Visitor

The snow fell softly and voices were hushed in the whiteness.

Beinn Ghuilean wore a white sheet.

Outside the ward the world waited for Christmas and birth, as I waited for a life to end.

There were carols in the streets and lights and decorations, which I found unreal and unnerving.

It was so much safer in the hospital. There was no need to pretend to be cheery, and no need to hide the tears which stung my eyes.

I was relatively familiar with death, having lost friends, relations and my much-loved father.

However, I had never met death, and that's the difference.

I had never sat with life and waited for this inevitable and unwelcome visitor who would come all too quickly and take my beloved mother to a place I didn't know.

I couldn't even ask him the questions that so burned within me.

Yet I sat and waited.

I rewound the video of my life, and put the pause button on at all the good bits. Sometimes laughing, often weeping, I walked and talked with my mother through 60 years and gave thanks for the gift of memory.

The ward was my sanctuary, the nurses my companions and the doctor my anchor.

I was on a bridge between the real world and the anteroom of death, and I actually wanted to be in the anteroom.

The anteroom of death became a place of life and honesty and blessing, as I shared the last precious days with the one who had given me the gift of life.

Gradually mum slipped off somewhere I couldn't reach her. Conversation was now one-sided, but still real.

Did death come in stages to torment us, or to prepare us?

Is that line between life and death really as thin as a gossamer thread? Does death actually occur in a heartbeat, or rather lack of it?

I sat and watched and waited and wondered. I waited for this unwelcome visitor and dreaded him. I dreaded him because I knew his purpose, and I dreaded him because he would rob me not only of my mother, but also of my control.

I had always 'fixed' things for mum, but this I couldn't fix.

I could only wait and watch and wonder.

I didn't know what to expect in these final stages. I was uneasy about the rattled breathing and the fluttering heartbeats.

I didn't like the impotence of my situation.

Yet in some strange way I was empowered by being there, by having the privilege to wait.

I had the privilege to see my mum cared for with dignity and compassion.

I had the unconditional acceptance and comfort and freedom to be myself.

But, I didn't like the rattle of death. This visitor was getting too close for comfort.

The snow fell fast and my world was on whiteout.

Where was my mum in this rattling chest and laboured breathing?

She was like a bird fluttering at a window wanting her freedom.

If only someone could open the window and let her go.

The visitor came in quietly as on the wings of a dove.

He didn't scare me, or mum, and he left just as silently.

I watched the pulse on her neck stop, and by the time I kissed her cheek she was already on the other side of time.

The snow still fell.

It was Christmas Eve.

Birth and death became one and the same.

Marilyn Shedden

In memory of Jenny, Salvationist and Anglican

She became transparent,
light as paper,
really very little left to die.
The radiant smile
already seemed much larger than the body,
filling the little bedroom with soft light.
Nurses listened for her breath
each time they came to turn her.
Scarcely audible,
but yes, still here, this time.
Did anyone witness, I wonder,
the delicate passing of this soldier saint?

Liz Gregory-Smith

Vigil

Nothing to say.
Nothing to do.
Only to sit
looking at you.

Nurses on tiptoe,
flowers blooming bright.
Watching you heading
into the Light.

Sun through the window,
whispers of talk.
Sand running slowly out,
end of the walk.

No need to worry.
We'll be all right.
We've got each other.
You go, to the Light.

A breath – and then silence,
the silence of dawn,
a blazing of sunshine,
we're left – and you've gone.

Catherine Harkin

For my mother

'Underneath are the everlasting arms':
loved words and loving,
reminding us of a God
who is always there,
like a mother with a young child,
knowing our needs,
catching us when we fall,
comforting, bearing, cradling, dancing and caressing.

Underneath are the everlasting arms:
words of encouragement
in moments of desolation
and loneliness;
words passed from mother to daughter,
not in cold print but warm with faith.

Underneath are the everlasting arms:
now you are dying
is it hard to let go?
For so long you have been there
to catch, to carry and to care.

Listen, love,
I want you to know
that I can cope:
first your faith nurtured me,
and your strength,
but now I have found my own.

Let go.
Into God's hands I commend your spirit.
Underneath are the everlasting arms.

Jan Sutch Pickard

Prayer at the time of death

God,
who holds all things together,
we commit to your loving care the life of *(name)*
and all *her/his* relationships with those
she/he loved in this life.

Help all who are gathered here to know
that all love in this life flows from your love,
a love that is stronger than death
and can never be quenched by it.

A life now returns to its source,
in safety and peace.
A life held in love.
Amen

James Curry

A life cut short

A hot summer's day.
I walk on the white strand.
Waves gently lap the shore,
gulls weave in and out over the sea;
a ringed plover runs over the sand,
an oyster catcher on a rock, at rest:
tranquillity, peace.

Across the Sound,
a mass of black surrounds a small kirk:
mournful farewell to a young soldier,
not yet 21, returning home –
never again to hear the rhythm of the sea,
to experience the tranquillity of the shore;
now finding his own peace.

Katherine Rennie

Messenger

February 10th 4am.
I take in my surroundings mechanically.
A clear yet starless night.
Crisp coldness.
Complete silence.
Inner landscape jangling and confused.
Telephone message. Hospital. Too late. Father dead.
Stomach churning.
I hear the car approach,
see her eyes searching for me in the half light.
Fumbling for the impossible,
a gentleness to all this,
I go to tell my mother.

Mary Hanrahan

With you

I had seen people dead before
but never so beautiful in death,
all your cares and worries smoothed away
by an unseen tender hand.

We gathered, all four of us,
daughters, 'adopted daughters'
who had cared for you so lovingly
in your final weeks and days.

We kissed you, laughed, wept,
fell silent, wanting to touch more
than your frail flesh, your silken cheek.
How could it be that you were gone?

Yet, had you not been gone,
we could not have given you
your final gifts, gifts to see you
safely to your home.

Another daughter's poem:
full of passion, tinged with longing,
wanting distances to shrink so
she could be here with us too.

A little paper plate
decorated just for you,
to enjoy the Royal Wedding,
my last day of life with you.

And Chelsea said, 'A hanky,
she always had a hanky.
She'll be lost without one now',
so we placed one on your breast.

What remains? Wee sweeties!
Two of your favourite chocolate éclairs!
To finish with a flourish!
Love is what remains.

Yvonne Morland

Nights and days (for Joanne)

You had no time to say anything:
Thank you
I love you
Bless you
not even Goodbye

By the time you reached the hospital
he'd gone;
his life,
and a huge part of yours,
was over.

The funeral was good.
People said what they needed to say.
There were tears, and anger and laughter.

His going
was not what either of you
would have wanted or imagined,
but it happened.

And you are left with sadness
and questions
and memories
and nights
and days.

Ruth Burgess

A phone call to Gary who died suddenly

Hi Gary,

You're not at home so I'm leaving a message on your answerphone – I hope I've pressed the right buttons or someone will be left a bit puzzled.

I'm not ringing with any special news but will ramble on anyway.

Gary, please tell me why you jumped the queue instead of waiting in line like the rest of us? I'm not the only one to be put out about it – and we'll have to discuss it sometime.

None of us talk much about our true feelings, do we? At our first meeting you looked me in the eye and I knew you were the right lad for our Joanne, and so it was proved. Loving, loyal, caring and calming, a very gentle man.

I was fortunate in having a similar model in my own life, and it is filled with memories.

Must stop rambling or the phone will cut out or something.

I send you a big hug and know that a bigger one will come back to me.

All my love and a huge thank you for being part of my family. I'd have been proud to call you: 'Gary, my son'.

Call me back when you can.

Love,
Rene

Irene Bruce

Before the funeral

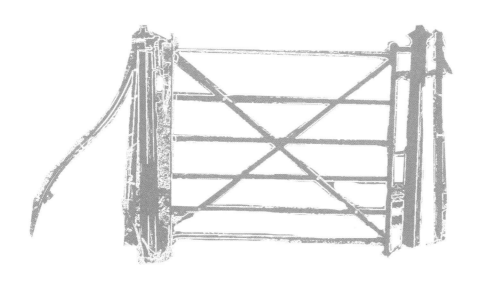

In the coffin

When my friend's mum died
she put a pair of ballet shoes
in her mum's coffin.

When my dad died
I put some runner beans in,
and autumn flowers and leaves.

Dreams for the journey,
harvest for the homecoming,
wonder for the way ahead.

When I die
my friends can choose for me –
something to sing would be good –
and I've always liked dandelions.

Ruth Burgess

Choosing a coffin

I like the idea
of a cardboard coffin
that could be decorated for me
by my family and friends.

Maybe it could be collaged.
They could choose pictures
of places that I've loved
and stick them on.

I'd like a dragon somewhere –
Welsh blood has always danced in me,
around my arteries
and veins.

And a Celtic cross …
and a fiery sun …

glitter and gold paint maybe,
and some crinkly foil stars …
I'm not ready to go yet,
you understand,
I'm just planting a few ideas
for when the time comes …

Ruth Burgess

Thank you for undertakers

Thank you God for undertakers.
Thank you for people who know their job.
Thank you for people who understand the paperwork.
Thank you for people who are familiar with grief.

Thank you God for undertakers.
Give them strength and wisdom and understanding.
Bless them with moments of wonder and laughter.
Keep them in integrity all their days.
Amen

Ruth Burgess

Dancing in the streets

When my time comes
please, please, please
no penguin parades,
no solemn posturing:
but folk in jeans,
children playing, babies crying
and dancing in the streets.

Ian M. Fraser

We wait

In quiet and in sadness
we wait.
With questions and anger
we wait.
With friends and with family
we wait.
We wait and we cry 'How long?' …

In the morning and the evening
we wait.
As the world goes on around us
we wait.
With an emptiness inside us
we wait.
We wait and we cry 'How long?' …

With the town of Machynlleth
we wait.
With our children and our neighbours
we wait.
With all who are sad and exhausted
we wait.
We wait and we cry 'How long?' …

Ruth Burgess, November 2012

This piece was written in response to a request for prayers from an Iona Community member living in Machynlleth, Wales, where a local child, April Jones, was abducted. At the time of the request the police had been searching for a number of weeks for her body.

Sealing a coffin

As I close the door on your earthly life,
may God open to you the gate of glory.

As your earthly life is sealed into death,
so may you rise with Christ.

May nails become
symbols of new life;
the wood that holds you,
symbol of salvation.

Kate McIlhagga

Names I do not know

It feels curious,
reading through your address book:
like visiting another country,
or reading a new poem.

There are names here that are fading,
names underlined,
names in green ink,
names of Welsh origin,
names written long ago.

There are names that are crossed out.
I puzzle.
Have they married and moved page?
Have they not returned a Christmas card?
Have they died or moved home?

There are a few names that I recognise,
family, current friends and neighbours,
but there are names and names that I do not know.

It feels odd, Mum,
reading through your address book,

knowing that I need to contact these strangers
to tell them that you have died.
Strangers to me, these people,
but not to you,
these people are part of your country, your story,
they may tell me things about you
that I do not know.

Ruth Burgess

Talking about you (for Trudy)

Talking about you
at your funeral
isn't going to be easy.

I want my words
to tell your story:
what made you laugh and cry
what made you angry
what made you you
what gave you hope.

I want to tell the story of your courage and wonder.
I want to remember the moments that filled your nights and days.

I want my memories to spark off the memories of others.
I want my words to be beginnings not endings.
I want to be true to who you were and are.

I want us to go on talking about you in the days to come.
I want your story to be alive in us:
your family, your friends, your community.

Talking about you
at your funeral
isn't going to be easy,
but I love you deeply
and I'm going to try …

Ruth Burgess

Gathering up treasure: a service for between a death and a funeral

In some Churches the body is brought into the church the night before a funeral. The following service could be used then. It could also be used in the home. It was originally written for an evening service of a church community after the death of their parish priest.

Opening responses:

Jesus said, 'I am the living bread come down from heaven:
anyone who eats of this bread will live forever.'
LORD, GIVE US THIS LIVING BREAD
AND DRAW US INTO YOUR ETERNAL LIFE.

Jesus said, 'I am the living water:
whoever drinks of me has a wellspring
welling up to eternal life.'
LORD, GIVE US YOUR LIVING WATER.
LET YOUR LIFE WELL UP IN US,
DRAWING US TO ETERNAL LIFE.

Jesus said, 'I am the Good Shepherd.
The shepherd who lays his life down for his sheep.'
LORD, BE OUR GOOD SHEPHERD.
WHEN WE WALK THROUGH VALLEYS OF SHADOW –
WHEN WE WALK THROUGH THE VALLEY OF DEATH –
BE WITH US WITH YOUR CROOK AND YOUR STAFF TO SUPPORT US,
AND LEAD US TO THE DAWN OF ETERNAL LIFE.

Jesus said, 'I am the gate of the sheepfold:
all who enter through me will be safe.'
LORD, WELCOME US THROUGH YOUR GATEWAY.
GUIDE US AND GUARD US
AND DRAW US INTO YOUR KEEPING IN ETERNAL LIFE.

Jesus said, 'I am the resurrection and the life:
anyone who believes in me shall live forever.'
LORD, WE BELIEVE –
HELP OUR UNBELIEF.
HELP US TO SEE IN YOU
OUR PROMISE OF RESURRECTION.
HELP US TO SEE IN YOU
OUR PROMISE OF ETERNAL LIFE.

Scripture reading: Matthew 6:19–21, 2 Corinthians 4:6–15

Reflection on the life of the person who has died:

People can be invited to share stories, and light candles in remembrance …

Closing responses:

We have gathered in your name, Lord.
BE WITH US IN OUR PARTING.

We have remembered and prayed for our *brother/sister (name)*
and for ourselves.
CHERISH OUR PRAYER, LORD,
COMFORT OUR GRIEVING
AND HONOUR OUR REMEMBERING:
ENFOLD OUR *BROTHER/SISTER* IN YOUR MERCY
AND BRING *HIM/HER* TO *HIS/HER* INHERITANCE OF ETERNAL LIFE.

We have remembered and gathered up treasures from the life of our *brother/sister*
and we place them in your keeping.
HOLD THEM,
BLESS THEM,
PLACE THEM IN THE ETERNAL TREASURY
FOR YOUR SERVANT TO FIND AS TREASURE
LAID UP IN HEAVEN –
WHERE NOTHING CAN DESTROY OR DIMINISH,
FOR ALL IS HELD IN YOUR GRACIOUSNESS
AND NOTHING THAT IS GOOD CAN BE LOST.

We pray for the week ahead,
with its joys and its sorrows,
for our community
and for those who will join us in mourning the passing of our *brother/sister (name)*.
MAY OUR CHURCH AND OUR HEARTS BE OPEN
TO WELCOME IN HOSPITALITY OUR GRIEVING BROTHERS AND SISTERS,
AND MAY OUR SORROW BE GENTLE
AS WE COMMEND OUR *BROTHER/SISTER*
TO THE TENDERNESS AND MERCY OF GOD.

We have gathered in your name, Lord.
BE WITH US IN OUR PARTING.

And so, may God bless us,
THE FATHER, THE SON AND THE HOLY SPIRIT.

And until we meet again
MAY GOD HOLD US IN THE PALM OF HIS HAND. AMEN

Wellspring

Stepping up a generation

It's strange
and scary
this stepping up a generation.

The realisation,
with the death of an aunt and mother,
that we
are now the elders –
that our family will look to us
for wisdom and support.

None of us look upon ourselves as old,
or particularly wise,
but we are the cousins and siblings
who hold the family story.
There is no one to go to now
to check that we've got it right,
no one but ourselves.

Maybe this is the time to compare notes.

Was it Uncle Bob or Uncle John who got chased by an elephant?
Was it Auntie Mary who met the king?
Who's got granddad's medals?
Who's going to look after Ada's tea service
and Lucy's silver thimble?

It's some responsibility
to hold the story
for our generation.

But we'll do our best
to keep it right.

Ruth Burgess

Resources for when children have died

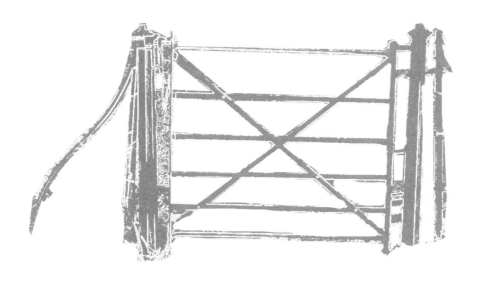

Rocking chair lament

My God, my God, why have you forsaken me?
Why am I all alone in this chair without my baby?
Its 2am, God – I should be in here feeding my child
and listening to the sound of her slumber.
Where are you, God? Where are you?
My body aches, my heart is broken,
and I don't think I can cry one more tear.
Where are you?
Why did this happen?
Why me?
How am I supposed to go on?
Will I ever sleep through the night again?
What about my husband?
Will he ever understand my pain?
Will we be okay?
Will this bring us closer?
He feels guilty for not feeling as bonded to her as I do.
Take that away from him, God.
We are still parents, right, God?
I'm still a mother and he's still a father, right?
O God, I cannot take this pain.
Take it away from me, God. Take it away.
Hold me, and rock me to sleep, God.
Hold me. Hold me.
Let me sleep.

A. A. Masters

Where were you?

God, what is she feeling?
I don't know how to help her feel better, God.
I don't know what to do.
I've never cried like this before.
I was just getting excited about this baby, God.
I'm ready to have someone call me Daddy.
I'm ready to have children.
I don't understand why this happened, God.
She did everything she was supposed to –
she ate right, exercised, went to the doctor and took vitamins.
What happened?
I don't know how to tell other people about this.
I wasn't prepared for this.
Why didn't you do something, God?
Why?
Where were you?
What am I supposed to do now?
What are we supposed to do now?
What if this happens again?
What if she never stops crying?
When will she physically feel better?
When will this pain go away?
When?
How much longer?
Are you listening?
Where were you?
Say something, God.
God?

A. A. Masters

Nursery prayer

As we gather in this nursery,
Lord, breathe life into this place.

As we fold these sheets and blankets and pack them away,
Lord, may we feel your warm embrace.

As we take this crib apart, piece by piece, section by section,
Lord, put the pieces of our hearts back together.

As we tuck the stuffed animals away into baskets,
Lord, comfort us with your gentle touch.

As we close the door to this nursery for a while,
Lord, remind us that yesterday, today and tomorrow
are in your hands.
Amen

A. A. Masters

Blessing of the mother's womb

O God, our Creator, our Parent, our Source of Life,
bless this mother as she grieves.
Take away her cramping.
Take away her bleeding.
Take away her pain.
Restore her body to health.
May she know that her body is beautiful
because she is made in your image.
May she know that she is valued
because she is your child.
May she know she is loved perfectly
and unconditionally.
Heal her body, God.
Heal her and make her whole again.
Amen

A. A. Masters

A blessing for twins who have died

God of all nations and children,
bless these precious twins of yours.
May they feel you holding them close
and may their bodies be restored to perfection.
Welcome them home with joy
and may they be soothed by the songs of angels.
Cradle these two boys in your arms, God,
since their parents cannot.

Bless their parents as they seek answers, God.
Embrace their parents as only you can
and breathe new life into their despair.
Bless their parents with the peace that surpasses all understanding
and the strength that can only come from you.
It is with broken and heavy hearts
that we give these boys back to you, God.
We give them back to you in the name of your child,
the Christ,
who welcomes all children home.
Amen

A. A. Masters

Funerals of babies and children

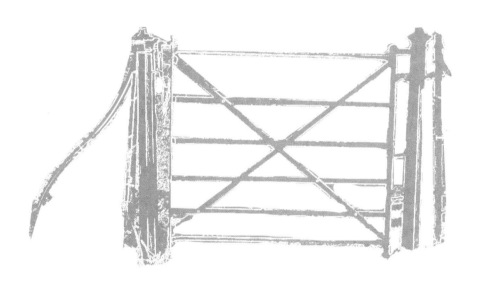

Liturgy for a stillborn child

As one whom a mother comforts
I will comfort you, says the Lord. (Isaiah 66:13)

We come here to thank God for *(name of child)*,
to thank God for *his/her* conception,
to thank God for the months *he/she*
was carried in *(name of mother)*'s womb
and in *(name of father)*'s heart;
to thank God that in *his/her* short life
he/she brought joy and laughter,
anticipation and hope for the future.

We gather to share our grief
and our anger that a life promised
has been taken; that hope seems
to have been cut off and joy destroyed.

We are here as *(parents, grandparents, friends and family …)*
to lay our questions,
our sadness and our hope
at the feet of Christ,
who opened his arms to receive
all who were wounded and distressed.

We have come to acknowledge
our feelings of guilt and failure,
and to affirm our conviction
that death is not the end,
but a new beginning.

Jesus says: *'Those who come to me,*
I will not cast out.' (John 6:37)

Those present are encouraged to give words to their hopes and fears, their anger, their sadness; to place flowers, poems, gifts, symbols of love and light on the coffin or on a nearby table.

A time of silence and of letting go

Chant: 'Be still and know' (from *There Is One Among Us*, John L. Bell, Wild Goose Publications) or 'Lord Jesus Christ, Lover of all' (from *Heaven Shall Not Wait*, John L. Bell and Graham Maule, Wild Goose Publications)

Prayer (said by all):

O God, as *(name of child)*
was cradled in the womb,
cradle *him/her* and hold *him/her*
that as we let *him/her* go,
we may know that *he/she* has gone
from our loving presence
into yours forever.
In Jesus' name we pray.
Amen

Kate McIlhagga

He was your son

What do I tell them?
Fifteen minutes is not long …
not exactly a lifetime –
yet it was.

The wedding was great!
The groom looked proud,
the bride looked beautiful,
the church was nearly full,
families and friends all there
and a great day of commitment and celebration.
A day of love,
of hope,
of looking forward,
of a new life together.

The baby was on the way!
Another time of love,
of hope,
of looking forward
and the promise of a new life.

Except …

Except the scans revealed problems.
       A hole in the heart –

and maybe other things too.
We'll need to wait and see.
We knew that all would not be well
for this particular little life.
Anxious days, worrying days.

The baby was born!
A day of love …
but not of hope
of looking forward,
and just a short young life.
Fifteen minutes – not long
but it was a lifetime.
Every new parent's secret nightmare now theirs for real.

The funeral was painful.
The father looked drawn,
the mother looked pained,
the church was empty,
just mother, father,
minister,
and undertaker holding a tiny white coffin
the size of a shoebox.

So what do I tell them?
What do I say to this grieving couple
whom I married not so long ago?
What can be said in the face of this nightmare?
What do I say
while looking this father, this mother in the face?

'He was your son.
 You loved him.
 He was your son.
 Be proud of him!'

David Hamflett

For the funeral service of an unborn baby

A and B: mother and father
C: the baby

As we meet here today our hearts are sad.
We come to offer our love and support to *(parents' names)*.
We join with them as they say their farewells to their *son/daughter/child,*
and as with love and care they lay C to rest.

C was conceived because of the love of A and B for each other.
Many of you will have happy memories of the months when A was carrying C.
There will be memories of hopes and plans and happiness.
Today, in our sadness, we still remember these months when C was living
and growing inside *his/her* mother.

We know that *his/her* life came to an end before it had completely begun.
We are sad at this.
We struggle to take it in.
Sometimes our sadness seems to completely overwhelm us.

But today, while we know that C was taken from A and B,
we affirm how important C was, how loved *he/she* was
and how much *his/her* birth was looked forward to.

In preparing for today, A and B have chosen two poems …

Poems are read …

Prayer:

We ask God to surround C with his love;
to take C into his arms and to take care of *him/her* for us
until the day when we shall see C again in heaven.

In the quietness, we each offer our own prayers.
God of love, hear our prayers …

Let us pray for A and B:
let us ask God to give them strength to get through today,
and to get through tomorrow,
and to get through every tomorrow.
God of love, hear our prayers …

Let us give thanks for the love of family and friends.
Let us ask God to help us all to support A and B and their families.
God of love, hear our prayers …

Hear all our prayers.
In Jesus' name we pray.
Amen

The committal (at the cemetery):

We have entrusted C to the love of God.
And we now gently lay to rest *his/her* little body in the quiet earth.

Earth to earth, ashes to ashes, dust to dust.
But we do this in the sure and certain hope of the resurrection to eternal life,
through Jesus Christ our Lord.

And now may God's peace,
God's love
and God's strength
be with each one of you
and all those whom you love,
today,
tomorrow
and every tomorrow,
for evermore.
Amen

Ken Russell

Firstborn

My little one – you would have been my firstborn
but I will never really know you,
for I was never destined to hold you in my arms,
to watch you smile and see you grow,
to feel your softness and smell your sweet baby smell,
for you were lost to me almost before I knew you.

And yet we shared things, didn't we?
My hands rested on my stomach and imagined they could touch you

and I smiled in that first secret knowledge of you.
I remember watching snowflakes and telling you about their beauty –
as if you didn't know already!
Tears did nothing to relieve the loss I felt when you were gone.
I will never believe people who tell me
'You cannot love a child so soon,'
for I love you,
and regret what might have been and which is lost.

But now, at last, with the love of Christ,
my unspoken grief is healed
and I can say to you, with love,
be at peace my precious baby – my firstborn.

Christine Green

The moment

The moment we knew about you
we loved you.

The moment you kicked in the womb
we loved you.

The moment we first saw you
we loved you.

The moment we held you in our arms
we loved you.

The moment we called you by your name
we loved you.

(Child's name)
we love you and we always will.

Ruth Burgess

Stillborn: a liturgy

Prayer:

God of all grace and comfort,
you made each of us beautiful in your own image;
you love us from the day you create us from your good earth,
moistened with your breath of life.

We thank you, O God, for *(name)*,
for giving *her/him* an everlasting place in our hearts.

We thank you for being with us
each day of our existence:
in plenty and in want,
in joy and in sorrow,
in sickness and in health.

Dear God, you know all our thoughts and feelings.
When we forget the meaning of life,
recall in us your purpose for our lives:
to glorify you and enjoy you forever.
When we feel lost and afraid,
remind each of us who we are:
a human being in whom you trust.
Strengthen our hearts to love,
open our minds to imagine,
exercise our souls to believe,
inspire our bodies to practise your Shalom,
your Salaam, your peace.
Amen

Hymn of assurance: (e.g. 'When we are living, we are in the Lord', Mexican traditional, Roberto Escamilla and John L. Bell, CH4)

Scripture reading: Psalm 23, NRSV, made inclusive:

The Lord is my shepherd –
I shall not want!
Who makes me lie down in green pastures,
who leads me beside still waters,
who restores my soul,
who leads me in paths of rightness

for God's own sake.
Even though I walk through
the valley of the shadow of death,
I fear no evil
for you are with me.
Your rod and your staff –
they comfort me.
You prepare a table before me
in the presence of all my fears.
You anoint my head with oil.
Surely goodness and mercy
will follow me all the days of my life,
and I will dwell in the house of the Lord forever.

Sermon/homily:

(Name), daughter/son of *(name/s),*
was born and died on *(day/date)* at *(place).*
Not every person's life has a middle part,
but each person's life has a beginning and an end.
Live assured,
this child's life began and ended as described by the Psalmist:
The Lord was and continues to be *her/his* shepherd –
(Name) lacks for nothing.
God laid *her/him* down and nourished *her/him* in *her/his* mother's body
and wrapped *her/him* in the waters of the womb.
Her/his soul is stored with God,
and *she/he* dwells in God's heavenly abode forever.

For those of us whose lives do have a middle part,
we will get through this hour and the next hour –
the coming days and weeks, months and years –
because it is God who leads us through our grief,
and God knows intimately what we're going through:
God lost a child.

Even though we walk through the valley of the shadow of death,
we need fear no evil for God is with every one of us.
God's rod and staff – they are there to comfort us.
God even goes so far as to prepare a meal for us
in the presence of our fears,
our anger, our depression,

our overwhelming sense that life can't go on.
God showers us with tears,
restoring courage to our souls,
opening our hearts to enjoy again,
anointing our minds with fresh peace,
bringing our bodies around.
Each of our lives comes full circle,
no matter how small that circle is.
(Name) belongs to God.
You belong to God.
We all belong to God.
Amen

Hymn of thanksgiving: (e.g. 'God, our help in ages past', excluding verse 5)

The following may be conducted at the burial:

Prayer of thanksgiving (based on Psalm 121, NRSV):

Dear God, I lift up my eyes to the hills and wonder,
from where will my help come?
Our help comes from you, O God,
who made heaven and earth.
You, who will not let our feet be moved.
You, who keep us, will not slumber.
You, who keep the whole world,
will neither slumber nor sleep.
Thank you, dear God, for being our keeper,
for being the shade at our right hand.
The sun shall not strike by day,
nor the moon by night.
Keep us from all evil; keep our lives.
Keep our going out and our coming in
from this time on and for evermore.

All our prayers we give to you, O God,
by the power of your Holy Spirit,
and by the grace of your Child Jesus Christ,
who teaches us to pray, saying …

The Lord's Prayer

Committal:

We commit *(name)*,
daughter/son of *(name/s)*,
and a child of God,
to God *her/his* Creator.

Benediction:

Do not worry about anything,
but in everything by prayer and supplication with thanksgiving
let your requests be made known to God.
And the peace of God, which surpasses all understanding,
will guard your hearts and your minds in Christ Jesus.
Amen *(Philippians 4:6–7, NRSV)*

Lindsay Louise Biddle

Baby blessing and naming after death

Prayers:

Loving God, be with *(parents' names)* in their grief over their baby's death.

May they be close to one another,
support one another,
care for one another,
comfort one another
and grow in love and understanding together.

Creator God,
be with us as we face the mystery of life and death.
Strengthen the bonds of this family as they bear their loss.
Help them to go on from here
with courage and confidence in your care and love.
Amen

Naming:

(Name), *I/we* give you this name,
knowing that you are a child of God,
Father, Son and Holy Spirit.

Blessing:

Unto God's gracious care we commit *(name)*.

May the Lord bless you and watch over you,
may the Lord make his face to shine upon you,
may the Lord look kindly on you and give you peace,
now and forever.
Amen

The Lord's Prayer

Kes Grant

Funeral for when a twin dies and a twin survives

Baby S – the child who has died
Baby T – the child who has survived

We have come together to remember Baby S in the presence of God. We come to say goodbye, and to entrust *her/him* into God's loving care and protection.

We perhaps feel many things: thanksgiving for *her/his brother/sister* T; sadness and devastation at the death of Baby S.

A time of joy and happiness was expected, and now there is pain and tears. Our minds are full of questions to which there appear to be no answers: so many things we do not know; so many things we do not understand.

There are no easy answers, but we can trust that God is with Baby S, and each one of us, from the moment of conception, and in life, death and beyond to eternity. Perhaps today is about being with our feelings of rawness and incompleteness.

Prayer:

Heavenly Father,
your Son took little children into his arms
and blessed them.
Grant to us now the assurance that both Baby S and Baby T
are encircled by those arms of love.
In the midst of our grief
strengthen our faith and hope in your Son,
Jesus Christ our Lord.
Amen

Readings: Mark 10:14–17, Psalm 127, stories, poems …

Gentle music/touching the coffin

Prayer:

Heavenly Father, your love for all your children is strong and enduring. We were not able to know Baby S as we had hoped. Yet *she/he* is known to you. In the midst of our sadness we thank you that we can trust *she/he* is with you now.

God our Creator, comfort this family, especially parents *(names)* grieving for the loss of their hoped-for child, and be with *her/his brother/sister*. Help them all to find the reassurance that with you nothing is wasted or incomplete, and uphold them with your love.

God of hope, we come to you with all our grief and confusion of heart. Help us to trust in your goodness and wisdom when our understanding fails. Help us to find peace in the knowledge of your loving mercy to all your children, and give us light to guide us out of our darkness into the assurance of your love.

The Lord's Prayer

Commendation:

We remember, Lord, the slenderness of the thread which separates life and death, and the suddenness with which it can be broken. Assure us that when those we love die, neither they nor we are separated from you, and in that assurance may we find peace.

Let us commend S to the love of God our Father:

To you, gentle Father, we humbly entrust *(child's full name)*, so precious in your sight. Take *her/him* into your arms and welcome *her/him* into your presence, where there is neither sorrow nor pain, but the fullness of peace and joy with you forever and ever …

We have entrusted Baby S to God's mercy, and we now commit *her/him* to be buried – earth to earth, ashes to ashes, dust to dust – in sure and certain hope of the resurrection to eternal life through our Lord Jesus Christ. Amen

Blessing:

May Christ the Good Shepherd enfold you with his love,
fill you with his peace and
lead you in hope this day and all your days.

And the blessing of God Almighty,
the Father, the Son and the Holy Spirit,
rest upon and remain with you,
this day and always.
Amen

Kes Grant

Balloons and doves: a sudden death of a child

Gathering:

We've come together to remember *(name of child)* in the presence of God. We come to celebrate *his/her* short life, to grieve, to say goodbye and to entrust *him/her* into God's loving care. Our hopes and dreams have changed because *(name)* has died. We feel a deep sense of loss and diminishment, and a need to support one another in our grief. But we also come with a feeling of thanksgiving for the many ways in which *(name)* has touched our lives. For the immediate family *(name)* was and is extra special. But *he/she* touched us all and we think and feel differently because of the difference *he/she* made to us. And today, and here in this place, *(name)* is linking us all together in grief. And yet grief goes hand in hand with love. In whatever way we express grief, it shows our love for *(name)*. And surely that's the most important thing for any human being, of whatever age: simply to be loved.

Words recalling the child's life (from the parents, relatives, friends …)

Prayer:

Heavenly Father,
your Son took little children into his arms
and blessed them.
Grant to us now the assurance that *(name)* is encircled
by those arms of love.
In the midst of our grief
strengthen our faith and hope
in your Son, Jesus Christ our Lord.
Amen

The Lord's Prayer

Prayers:

God of all grace and comfort, we thank you for *(name)* and for the place *he/she* has gained in all our hearts. We thank you for the love and care with which *he/she* was surrounded. As we remember times of tears and of laughter, we thank you for the love we shared because of *him/her,* and we commend *(name)* to your safekeeping. Grant eternal rest unto *(name)*. Let light perpetual shine upon *(name)*.

We give thanks to God for all who cared for *(name)* in any way: for the extended family, for health care professionals and for loving friends and family.

God our Creator, comfort *(names of parents, grandparents, great-grandparents, aunts, uncles, cousins …)*, each grieving their loss. Help them to find reassurance that with you nothing is wasted or incomplete, and uphold them with your love.

God, we are told that you are compassionate: today this is hard to believe.

God, we are told that you love us: today we do not feel loved.

God, we are told that we should offer you our praise and thanksgiving: today all we have to offer is anger and confusion.

God, despite these feelings we turn to you: today there is no one else to turn to.

God, hold us until we can believe again.

God, love us until we can feel your love again.

God, accept our anger and confusion until we can offer you praise and thanksgiving again.

God, our lives and our feelings rise and fall but you remain constant.

Help us to rest in your eternal changelessness.
Amen

Invitation:

I invite you to recall *(name)* and to hold *(him/her)* in your memory – all the things that made *(him/her)* a special and unique human being – and to come and touch the coffin in a final act of saying goodbye.

Prayer:

Each sunrise
each sunset
we will remember *(name)*.
As long as we live
he/she lives too
for *(name)* is now
and always
a part of us.

(Adapted from a Jewish funeral prayer)

Commendation and committal:

Let us commend *(name)* into God's loving care.

To you, gentle Father, we humbly entrust *(child's full name)*, so precious in your sight. Take *him/her* into your arms and welcome *him/her* into your presence, where there is neither sorrow nor pain, but the fullness of peace and joy with you forever and ever. Amen …

We have entrusted *(name)* to God's mercy, and we now commit *his/her* body to be cremated – earth to earth, ashes to ashes, dust to dust – in sure and certain hope of the resurrection to eternal life through our Lord Jesus Christ. Amen

Act of farewell:

We affirm that none of us lives in vain, labours in vain, gives or receives love in vain. Within the love of God each of us is worth more than we can ever calculate. For all the ways *(name)*'s life touched and enriched ours, we give thanks to God.

Release of balloons and doves and blessing:

As we watch the balloons rise up in the sky
WE LET YOU GO.
As we watch the doves fly into the distance
WE LET YOU GO.
Into the mystery and love of God
WE LET YOU GO.

May the love of God and the peace of the Lord Jesus Christ console us,
and gently wipe the tears from our eyes.

And the blessing of God Almighty,
the Father, the Son and the Holy Spirit,
be upon you and remain with you.
Amen

Kes Grant

Losing you

Words
Carol Dixon & Colin Dixon

Music
Colin Dixon & Simon Dixon

Losing you (song for Nicola)

I can't find the words to say how much I miss you,
your gentle smile and soft brown eyes so kind,
the way you walk and wear your hair;
the sunshine of your presence fills my life.

It hurts so much to think that I have lost you,
I guess I should remember the good days;
their memories will take away
this aching void I feel, knowing you've gone.

I recall the happy days when you were with me,
then suddenly you were taken away.
I can't believe you've really gone –
we never had the time to say goodbye.

One day I know that we will be together,
and then I'll tell you what you mean to me;
the hope we shared, the fun we had,
is with me always, and I'll see you again,
I'll see you again.

* Dedicated to the memory of Nicola Dixon, aged 17, murdered in Sutton Coldfield, 31 December, 1996

Words: Carol and Colin Dixon
Music: Colin and Simon Dixon

Remember

You love him. That's why you feel like this.
That will never change.

Without you he wouldn't have discovered life,
enjoyed learning,
driven you crazy as he strained in adolescence to gain his independence,
while needing you more than he would admit, or you could know.
And still he needs you, in spite of his death.
In death as in life, he is your child,
to be remembered with all the love
you ever had for him,
with all the frustration he brought you,
as well as the joy and privilege of parenthood.
Love him still.

Always love him.
Talk about his birth, his life, his ups and downs.
Talk of success and failure.
Talk of love and frustration.
Talk about him.
And never, never let him go.
He is your son.
He was and is and always will be.
The joyful pain of knowing that will live with you forever.
Every day you will picture him,
hear his voice
and ask the unanswerable 'what ifs',
until that point when it registers that,
in spite of all that has happened,
nothing, but nothing,
can separate you, or him, from God's love …

Even now you are still a uniquely valued child of God.
God hurts with you,
cries with you,
holds you,
enfolds you with love.
And you are safe.
Nothing can harm you any more.
Your memories are safe and the love in which you are held is eternal.

So rest in that love of God that will never,
never let you go.

Andrew Pratt

Funerals of adults

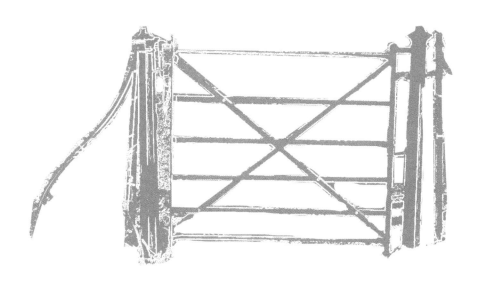

Funeral at a crematorium

Music

Scripture passages: spoken as people walk in carrying the coffin; not all the passages will be used:

God's love is not exhausted, nor has God's compassion failed. (Lamentations 3:22)

God cares for you, so cast all your anxiety on God. (1 Peter 5:7)

God is our refuge and our strength, a very present help in trouble. (Psalm 46:1)

Peace is my parting gift to you: my own peace, such as the world cannot give. Set your troubled hearts at rest, and banish your fears. (John 14:27)

I saw a new heaven and a new earth; for the first heaven and the first earth had vanished. I saw the holy city, the new Jerusalem, coming down out of heaven from God ... and I heard a loud voice proclaiming: 'Now God has his home with humankind. He will dwell among them and they shall be his people and God himself will be with them. He shall wipe away every tear from their eyes. There shall be an end to death, and to mourning and crying and pain, for the old order has passed away.' (Revelation 21:1–4)

Opening:

Friends, we are here to mourn and celebrate the life of N.
We have a job to do today, and a longer task to get underway.
First, to acknowledge the shock of N's death.
Then we should take the time and space we need to say goodbye.
We seek the Good News of God at work in the _____ years
it was given to John to share with us.
And then we seek to find healing and peace
to enable the bereavement process to move on.

Let us share the quiet of this place ...

Let us pray:

Enfold us, Lord, within your comforting arms.
Help us to feel at home, even though we are hurting.
Help us to know that we are not alone,
that we need have no fear of being human,
of showing how we feel,
for you know the pain of our loss.

Enfold us with courage.
Help us not to hold back the questions, the hurt or confusion.
May we know that through your grace
we may find rest within the circle of your love.

Hymn or song

Reflection by a family member or a friend

Reading/s from scripture

Address

Prayers for those who grieve:

Almighty and intimate God, you start where we are:
with doubts, with faith, with anger, with resignation,
and you surprise us when you accept in us
what we cannot even acknowledge to ourselves.
You know us better than we know ourselves,
and, by your grace, all things may be healed.
So we pray:

Make your peace
in us and amongst us,
that we ourselves may be made whole,
through Jesus Christ,
our Saviour and our friend.

Silence

Help us to confess any hurt or wrong we feel we have done to N,
or to let go of any hurt or wrong we feel *she/he* has done to us.
Help us to know that we are forgiven, that we need carry burdens no longer,
for Christ calls us to forgive others and to forgive ourselves, for God forgives us.

Silence

Living, loving God, give us joy deeper than sorrow
as we thank you for all your children,
and especially for N,
whom we now commit into your care and keeping,
knowing that *she/he* is safe and surrounded by the warmth of your love.

Silence

Let us pray for N's family and friends, and for all who cared for N.
May they be enabled to grieve now, but not as those without hope.
For you offer peace, joy, healing:
gifts that no one, and no grief, can take away.
Help us to cope with the pain and to remember with joy.
Though we may feel very alone – God is with us.
Though we may feel overwhelmed – God is with us.
Though we may wonder how we will cope – God is with us.
God is in our past and in our future,
in our fears and in our hopes,
in our tears and in our laughter.
God surrounds us and enfolds us with love, light and peace.

We trust that beyond absence there is a presence.
That beyond the pain there can be healing.
That beyond the brokenness there can be wholeness.
That beyond the anger there may be peace.

The Lord's Prayer (said together; allow for a variety of forms)

Poem

Hymn or song

Committal:

Invite people to come and lay a hand on N's coffin to say goodbye.

After all have come, lay a hand on the coffin and say:

So we send you forth, N,
upon your journey from this world:
set free in the love of God the life-giver,
in the compassion of Jesus,
who walks with you,
in the power of the Holy Spirit,
who enfolds you and us
here and now.

God of all hope –
living God above us, beneath us, behind us and before us –

having commended our friend N to your care,
we commit *her/his* body to be cremated –
earth to earth, ashes to ashes, dust to dust –
placing our trust and confidence
in the mercy and love of God
and in the solidarity and new life of his Son Jesus Christ,
our Lord who died,
was buried
and rose again
to live for us.
And we take comfort in the Holy Spirit
who is with us here and now,
and in all that lies ahead.

Lord, we do not know whether our days will be many or few.
Help us to put into each day's living something of worth and kindness,
integrity, courage and love.
These are the signs of your Spirit at work among us.

So Lord, we hold out to you all who have gathered here today.
May those who have suffered loss know the comfort of friendship and love.
And may this time of grief and mourning lead to a time of healing and peace.
For with you all shall be well, and all manner of things shall be well.

Blessing:

Deep peace of the running wave to you,
deep peace of the flowing air to you,
deep peace of the quiet earth to you,
deep peace of the shining stars to you,
deep peace of the Son of Peace to you.

And the blessing of God, the Holy Trinity,
guard and guide you,
now and evermore.

Music

Zam Walker

In memoriam JSB (1915–2008)

Some pictures of a life:

apprehensive at the dame school in big boots and leggings,
in the backyard with cousins and the dog, and father the year before he died,
serious studio portrait with brothers, on the threshold of adult life,
wedding day in haste as war loomed,
'Grand National' over the new privet with son in the saddle,
retirement do with happy colleagues,
trademark flowery tie at the golden wedding,
solitary in widowhood, cheating on the quick crossword with the thesaurus,
cheerful 90th birthday, thanks to friends and neighbours,
last days in the care home with grandson and granddaughter-in-law to be.

Lord, I hold before you:
a serious son,
a devoted brother,
a loving husband,
a considerate father,
an innovative colleague,
a caring and respected boss,
a mild and gentle old man.

I give you thanks for a long life lived well,
seeking your kingdom.

May he rest in peace and rise in glory.

Nick Burden

Funeral service in a church

Introduction:

We have gathered today to worship God, to give thanks for the life of X, and to express our loving sympathy and support for *his/her* family and friends.

Every death of course carries with it feelings of sadness and loss, and we come to share these feelings with one another before God. We grieve at X's parting from among us, and yet at the same time we give thanks for a long life lived well – faithfully and lovingly. And we praise God that, in completing *his/her* earthly life and passing through the mystery of death, X is at peace, fulfilled and made whole in God's nearer presence.

Praise to God the Father of our Lord Jesus Christ. In his great mercy, by the raising of Jesus Christ from the dead, he gave us new birth and living hope.

Hymn

Prayer:

Eternal God, you are the ground of our hope, the wellspring of our joy: we praise you for your creative and constant love that surrounds us and sustains us through all the passing ups and downs of our lives.

Jesus Christ, you came among us full of grace and truth: we praise you for your compassion for all who reach out to you.

Holy Spirit, you inspire and comfort us: we praise you for your guidance when we are uncertain, your challenge when we need to move on.

Gracious God, at this time of both thanksgiving and sadness, we grieve at the passing of X from among us; we celebrate *his/her* attainment of fullness of life beyond death; and we reflect on our own journey of faith.

We want the world to be a better place: we seek a better life for ourselves and for other people. You have shown us your way of compassion, generosity and justice in Jesus Christ; we know your will and the promises of your kingdom. You know our good intentions and deep desires, and you know too when we go astray. We bring before you those parts of our lives in need of your forgiveness and transforming grace – where our eyes have been blind, our hearts have been hard, our words or thoughts harsh, our lives preoccupied with the wrong things.

Loving God, whose promise is to make all things new, grant us your mercy, release us from any burden of shame or guilt we bear, strengthen us in your service to care for others, fill our hearts with your love and our lives with your glory and peace, through Jesus Christ our Lord. Amen

Readings

Tribute

Prayer:

Living God, we thank you for every glimpse and intimation of your love breaking into our world. We thank you for our belonging together in the household of faith, called to share in the building of your kingdom and to worship and witness to your glory. We thank you for all the experiences and people who have influenced and shaped our lives for good.

Above all, today we give thanks for X – for the privilege of knowing *him/her*, for *his/her* special gifts of character and personality, above all for the love *he/she* gave and received as *(husband, father, grandfather, uncle and partner; wife, mother, grandmother, aunt and friend)*. We thank you for all the good things in X's life and all the good times and the happy and helpful memories of X, and for all those others who have gone before us in the faith.

Loving God, grant us your grace that we too may come to know the fullness of eternal joy; but for now help us, in our own situations and circumstances, to share in the ministry of Jesus Christ, bringing reconciliation to those who are divided, strength to those who are weary, justice to those who are oppressed, and hope to those who are lost. Bless us and all your people with energy and vision, and great joy in serving and believing, that we may live out our faith with courage and cheerfulness, compassion and zeal.

We pray for the trouble spots of the world, the places in the headlines, and those places where people are enduring suffering unknown. We remember those caught up in conflict or ground down by violence and injustice: may your peace prevail and your justice roll down like an ever-flowing stream.

And we pray for those who mourn X's death, for *(names)*, and for all the wider circle of family and friends.

Loving and generous God, may your healing hopeful love strengthen, encourage and bring relief to all those people and places we have prayed for. And as we go forth from this place, may the spirit of thanksgiving and celebration be alive in our hearts, that in all that we say and do and are we may reflect the inspiration and example of those who have gone before us, and embody your loving purpose for all. We ask this in Jesus' name to whom be glory, now and for evermore. Amen

Hymn

Benediction

Norman Shanks

Committal at a crematorium

A short while ago we gathered in *(name of church)* to give thanks for the life of X. And now we are here for this second stage of *his/her* funeral.

I am not going to repeat what was said at the church. Each of you here has your own very personal recollections to treasure and reflect on at this time and over the days ahead. As we share the complex emotions we have at this time and honour and give thanks in worship to God for X's life, we reach out beyond whatever doubts and uncertainties we may have, to hear once more the good news of God's steadfast love, sure even in the darkest and most stressful times. We come to be comforted by the message of resurrection that tells us that death is not the end and that we may be strengthened in hope and enabled ourselves to face death without fear or bitterness or guilt.

Hymn (optional)

Prayer *(adapt as necessary)*:

The eternal God is your dwelling-place and underneath are the everlasting arms. Blessed are those who mourn for they shall be comforted.

Let us pray:

Gracious God, we offer you thanks and praise that in Jesus Christ you have opened up for us the way of abundant life and ever-new possibilities. In his life and death you have revealed your way and shown that your love has no limits; by raising Jesus from the dead you have made real the promise that each of us may share in the resurrection life.

Living God, we give thanks for all our friends and loved ones in whom we have glimpsed and experienced the light of your presence, the challenge of your justice and the warmth of your love. Especially today we give thanks for X: for *his/her* long and active life, for *his/her* attractive, cheery, courteous personality, for *his/her* steadfast faith and commitment to the church. We thank you for everything in X that revealed the depth and energy of life, the strong sense that people matter and that life has meaning and purpose; we thank you for the privilege and pleasure of knowing *him/her;* and for the assurance that death is the gateway to a fuller life: that *he/she* is safe now in your keeping, your earthly work in *him/her* complete. And to your name be the glory now and forever. Amen

Reading (optional)

The committal:

God is our light and our salvation, and the stronghold of our lives: whom shall we fear?

We entrust X to God's loving care. Rest eternal grant unto *him/her*, O God; and let light perpetual shine upon *him/her*. We now commit *his/her* body to be cremated – ashes to ashes, dust to dust – in sure and certain hope of the resurrection to eternal life through Jesus Christ, who died, was buried and rose again for us. Amen

Closing prayer:

Loving God, we remember with concern and affection those whose sense of loss is keenest because their love was deepest and most personal: we remember especially *(names)*, and all the wider circle of family and friends. Let their feelings of loss, sorrow and pain be transformed by hope. May they know the strength of your love that passes understanding and will not let them go; and by your grace, through the support they give one another and get from those around them, help them to face the days ahead with courage and hope.

God of love, may your strength and compassion be near and real to us all at this time. Help us to live our lives within your love, with a sensitivity and commitment to the needs of others. Give us grace to face life's tasks and challenges with steady nerves, a calm heart and a courageous spirit that we may be truly worthy of those who have gone before us and enriched our lives so much. Amen

Blessing:

Go forth in peace, and the blessing of God, Father, Son and Holy Spirit, be with you all, now and for evermore. Amen

Norman Shanks

Some words spoken at the funeral of a young man murdered in Glasgow

Let me offer three thoughts as we prepare to worship God.

The sheet you have in your hands says that this is a service of thanksgiving for John. Can we be sure that, despite the tragic circumstances of his death, we take this opportunity to be grateful for the whole of John's short life: as a child, as a wee boy, as a young adult, as a son, as a brother, as a fiancé, as a friend? John was, and is, far more than just the tragedy of his death.

The sheet you have in your hands says that this is a service of thanksgiving. Can we be sure to remember who we are thanking? We're thanking God for John. And this God is not some far-off big man in the sky. This God is not a big meanie way up there, who is somehow to blame for John's death. This God is the one who came among us in Jesus, died a cruel death for us and, we believe, rose from the dead. This is the God of life, the living God, who loves us – everyone: who weeps and suffers when we weep and suffer, and who at the end of the day we can trust to bring us through even the worst that life can do to us.

Lastly, the sheet you have in your hands says that John will never be forgotten. Inside, there are words written by his father, and his two sisters. Some of the words, especially in his dad's poem about violence, are angry words – they speak for us all. But the best way John will not be forgotten is surely if each person here commits themselves to working to root out the violence that caused John's death. It is we, the living, who must honour John by ensuring, as best as we can, that no more young men die on our streets the way John died. That way, John will not have died in vain. That way, John will not be forgotten. That way, we will truly give thanks for John's life …

John Harvey

Reflection at a graveside in Mull
(at the burial of Julia Wroughton, landscape artist)

At the turning of the year we gather here
to remember Julia, who made this island her home,
who relished the changeful beauty of its landscapes,
and reflected them in her art.

In the introduction to her exhibition 'Poetry of Place', she said:
'When I wake up in the morning and look out to sea,
I am always surprised to find the islands still there.'

With the people we love,
it often seems that they will always be there,
though that is never boring.
Every day brings the joyful surprises
of their constancy and their changefulness.
And then one day we wake and the landmarks are gone.
Those we love are no longer there in the same way.

Now we are here,
having brought Julia's body to its last resting place.
But look out to sea – the islands are still there.
The landscapes in which we live both shape us
and speak to us of something greater than ourselves.
They can also become images of our inner lives.
Lift up your eyes to the great presence of the Burg –
the way it falls seawards like a diving gannet.
Are the twin waterfalls flowing today, playing together?
Are they being blown back over its shoulder by the wind from the west?
As we stand here, we can imagine the dark cliffs of Gribun,
further round, or of Carsaig, which mirror these,
light dancing on the waters of the bay there,
shimmering through leaves in the summer,
picking out the patchwork of lichen on ancient walls.
Julia observed such things closely and celebrated them
in disciplined patterns of black on white or exuberant colour.

This world we live in – this particular place we stand in –
speaks to us of something greater and more enduring than ourselves,
but also as intimate and unique as our lives.
And artists can capture and express this for the wider community.

We are part of the landscapes in which we live,
but we are also part of communities: they shape us, too.
There is Mull's deep-rooted community,
within which Julia
helped nurture a creative community:
a place of welcome, of inspiration, encouragement,
conviviality round the table.
Gifted people who now live on Mull found their gifts
were recognised and flourished at this community.
They discovered Mull, and the place discovered them.

Community goes on happening.
There are three generations of a family here.
And friends. People making their own connections,
their own pictures, their own poem in this place.
And today we gather round the grave of Julia,
brought together by our common humanity
and by love, which lives on.

Jan Sutch Pickard

Not grave

Three hours ago
I did not want to be here:
about to lower you, my mother,
my birther, channel into the world,
into this dead space,
this hole in the ground,
with my decaying father, still
beneath your earthly form.
I wanted to scream, 'No,'
resisting my own downward way,
fearful of the end I may attain.

Now I lift the silken cord,
left hand guiding,
taking the strain,
right hand ready to let you
slip away. And slip you do,
gliding downwards till I feel
a catch, and you releasing me.
Still lower, the catch again
and me releasing you.
The final fall so soft,
borne by tender wings.

Not grave at all.

Yvonne Morland

Walking to the funeral

Walking to the funeral

It was a damp morning.
We walked together from the house to church.
Four generations, filled with love and much respect.
She was at the head of us, safe in the walnut box
from the January drizzle.
Three sisters and their brother,
individually loved and individually loving their mother,
three husbands and a wife,
eleven grandchildren, some with spouses,
three great-grandchildren
and a child as yet unborn.
It was a kind of dance,
solemn and very proud.
We paused behind the hearse
as the bearers took their place
to lift her through the metal gate,
carry her along the so familiar path
to the church's entrance porch.

The church service

We were not alone,
stepping through the old oak doorway.
The village had come inside
to greet her and bid farewell.
'I know that my Redeemer liveth',
hymns of praise she'd chosen,
tributes of thanksgiving in words and music,
tears flowing freely,

helium balloons held high.
'A great lady, passing.
A good way to die.'

At the grave

We placed her in the grave
she'd visited for sixteen years.
A grandson took the spade,
each threw our little handful
of fresh-dug earth to cover them.
She brought heaven with her all those years,
there's little doubt she'll do so still.

The wake

'How she would have loved the party,'
villagers and relations said.
Actually, it seemed she was right there
among the reunions and animated conversations
in the Half Moon Inn.
'An enlarged heart,' the specialist had said –
quite true,
and we miss her now
and hold her in our hearts.
Perhaps in God's grace they can grow larger too.

Liz Gregory-Smith

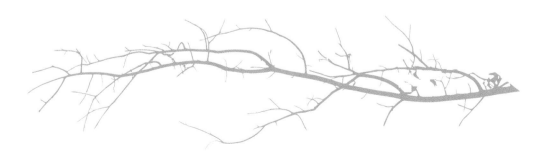

Letter from Vicky

I first met Vicky when she was 16. I was friends with her for four short years. During that time we became close, and I was privileged to help her plan her funeral. We looked at poems and readings. And she chose several pieces of music, all with a deep message: 'Three little birds (Everything's gonna be all right)', by Bob Marley, 'Don't worry, be happy', by Bobby McFerrin, and 'I did it my way', sung by Frank Sinatra. I had also talked to her about helping her write a letter, but being the very individual and wonderful person she was, she 'did it her way' and left this very moving letter for us (Kes Grant):

For everyone who knows me – well, if you're here you must know me – how silly am I? (Don't answer that.) Now, before I start, I just want you all to know, you're not getting away without me having my final say. (I bet you're all thinking: now there's a surprise.) I know you lot.

I want you all to know I had a great life. I couldn't have wished for a better one. I had the perfect mum and dad. I guess my brothers were OK (only kidding) – they were the best too! My life was different; sometimes it was hard but I had help from all my friends and family, not to mention help from two wonderful nurses, Peggy and Lance. I used to feel like giving up but I never did till now, but even then I didn't, it was my lungs, I blame them.

All of you CF [Cystic Fibrosis] kids/adults out there, you can do this – I know you can because you're strong. After all, now I'm not around, you need to take my place and keep all them nurses and doctors on their feet for me. Joking aside now: you *can* and *will* beat CF … Keep strong. I know you can do this, not only for me, but for yourself, friends and family; they are all there to help you. Don't let pride get in the way like I did. That's the biggest regret of my life, not letting people help me. Please don't do the same.

I'm OK up here with all my friends and family that I've lost in the past. In fact it's really peaceful, so I think I'll have to do something about that. Me and peace don't go together, as I'm sure you'll all agree. No doubt we'll all meet again on this side, and when we do – bring some good-looking men with ya – there are none here. Ha ha. This isn't the time for this kinda talk but what can I say, you miserable lots are making it sad and that's not what I want.

Well, I guess I should stop nattering on now and let you get on with the proper stuff. I just want to say one last thing: Thank you to everyone who was a part of my life. It was an honour to have you in it, and one last big thank you to my mum, dad, brothers, Lance, Kes and of course Peggy. You did a fantastic job. I love you all so much; and in case you think I'm not around, believe me I am. You might not be able to see or hear me but a part of me will always be with you all. You did all you could.

Vicky Dobbins

A simple funeral liturgy

I have often used this service during my ministry because I find that, for many people, ministry is more effective when the church uses a simplicity of liturgical style, most especially if the people concerned have little or no connection with the church. I always make it clear that I am a Christian minister but indicate that I believe it is both respectful and self-respecting when the church does not pretend a relationship which is not there. Obviously there are many adaptations to be made according to the honest realities of the person concerned.

I owe the idea of moving to touch the casket and the addressing of the person who has died to the Maori people of Aotearoa New Zealand. I have found that this diminishes the feeling of the lonely casket and also the 'untouchability' of death. Sometimes I have found it helpful to use this moment to tell the person who has died something which a member of the family wishes they had said to the person. For example 'Mary feels she never really told you how much she loves you. She does love you deeply, John.' Obviously, it is not helpful to take this too far. It is not meant to become a sort of confessional!

Opening:

Friends,
we have come together
because we loved *(name)*
as *(mother, brother, family, friend, etc).*
Here we will mourn *her/him* leaving us,
honour *her/his* life and death,
reverently farewell *her/his* body
and comfort each other.

We have come believing that all human life is valuable,
that the truth and integrity and hopefulness
which resides in each life, lives on.
We come, believing that *(name's)* life,
which we celebrate today
and for which we now experience great loss,
is joined in the eternal continuum of human endeavour
stretching into the past and into the future.

Her/his life was lived in its uniqueness with us
and has now passed into the ultimate community
of human existence.
The gifts and graces which *she/he* offered are never lost to us.
The creativity which *she/he* brought to us
in *her/his* life and relationships

lies now within our own lives
and travels into the future with us.
(If appropriate) Our lives are more beautiful because we lived with *her/him*.

Silent reflection, or prayer:

O God, at this moment,
as we come face to face with death
and our own mortality,
we have many feelings
as well as grief,
and possibly fear for the future.
Please come close to us with your love,
travel with us into this serious moment
and open our hearts to each other.
We ask it in the name of Jesus Christ
who faced his own death and the death of a friend.
Amen.

Lord's Prayer (if appropriate)

Readings (traditional and/or contemporary)

Reflection:

None of us know the whole truth about what lies beyond death.
Christians believe that as we journey between life and death,
we are safe in the hands of an infinitely gracious God.
We believe that death invites us into total awareness
and to know with truth whether what we have valued in ourselves has eternal value.
The God who stands with us at that moment
is the same God who was prepared to die in love for all humankind,
a God who has entered every struggle of our life with us
and who deeply understands the choices we have made.

Tribute (the things we would like to remember about the person):

The minister moves to the casket and placing a hand on it says:

(Name), all these things and more you have given to us.
We respect your journey through life,
with all of its realities.
We pray that you will travel safely
in this next part of your journey.

Our love goes with you.
Let us pray or reflect in silence on this life and what it has meant to us:
(silent prayer/reflection)

Thanks be to God for the gifts we have received in this person.
Thanks be to God for a life lived with *(courage, honesty, grace, determination – as appropriate).*

If a burial:

We will now accompany you to your final resting place.

(The casket is carried to the grave.)

The farewell:

As we come to the moment of farewell,
part of our grief may be regret
for things done or left undone,
words said, or never said,
or moments that never happened.
This is the time to lay aside all those regrets
and to honour the spirit of *(name) herself/himself*
who would never want them carried into our future.
Let us receive that gift of generosity from *(name)*
and the forgiveness of God.

(Silent reflection)

To love someone is to risk the pain of parting.
Not to love is never to have lived.
The grief which we now experience is the honouring of our love.

Let us now in a quiet moment
make our farewell to *(name)*

(Silence)

The committal:

If a burial:

And now let us commit *her/his* body to the earth
which is welcoming to us at the time of our death.
Ashes to ashes, dust to dust.
In the cycle of life and death the earth is replenished
and life is eternally renewed.

If a cremation:

And now let us commit *her/his* body to the elements
which are gentle to us at the time of our death.
Ashes to ashes, dust to dust.
In the cycle of life and death the earth is replenished
and life is eternally renewed.

Go in peace, *(name)*.
Travel safely with our love
into the hands of God.
Amen.

Blessing and dismissal:

Even as we grieve this loss,
let us commit ourselves to the comfort of those who miss *her/him* most
especially *(names)*.
Let us surround them with our love
and pray for the comfort of God.

And now let us go into the world,
glad that we have loved,
free to weep for the one we have lost,
free to hold each other in our human frailty,
empowered to live life to the full
(if appropriate) as did *(name)*
and to affirm the hope of human existence.
And may God be our company,
Christ Jesus walk before us
and the Spirit surround us with a cloud of grace.
Amen.

Dorothy McRae-McMahon

An order of service for a funeral

Call to remembrance:

Here in the presence of death, God is with us.

We have come here today to remember N:
to give thanks for *him/her*,
to try to find some comfort, some help to bear our loss.
We feel numb or angry, helpless and lost.
We need space and time to grieve and to remember.
Some of us need silence, quiet, to be alone.
Others need company and conversation.

There is no right or wrong way to feel when someone dies.
God can cope with all these things,
so let us share our feelings with God.

Let us pray:

God, in our vulnerability and loss
help us to hold one another in love.
Like a father, strengthen us.
Like a mother, comfort us.
Enable our tears.
Hear our sighs.
Help us to live through our doubt.
Teach us the truth that the darkness
has never overcome
the light of your love.
Help us to care for each other
and to love each other through this grief.
Amen

And now, O God, remind us of the faith
that has brought encouragement and reassurance
to your people over the years.

Bible readings: Ecclesiastes 3:1–8; Psalm 23; Psalm 121; Luke 12:22–31; John 14:1–3, 27; Romans 8:35, 37–39

These words speak of the experience of people in the past. We may, or may not, be able to make them our own. They may sound hollow or irrelevant. Come back to them again, in a month, in a year. Perhaps then they'll make sense. What is sure, is that the love of which the

Bible speaks is made real when we love each other. We become channels, instruments of God's love.

A remembrance (a tribute to the deceased):

Let us remember N.

You know N.
Picture *him/her* in your mind's eye.
Thumb through the photographs of your memory,
run again the film of the life you shared.
Remember the sunshine and the rain,
the laughter and the tears,
all that made N unique and special,
all that continues to keep *him/her* special for you now.

Silence

We remember N.
We thank you, God, for *him/her*.
We are grateful for all *he/she* has meant to us.
Help us to set aside the time when things went wrong,
for we are all human and make mistakes.
Help us to keep *him/her* alive by seeking to do the good things that *he/she* did,
to repeat to each other the kind words that were found on *his/her* lips.
We are thankful: our lives are different because we have known *him/her*.
We will never be the same again.

The Lord's Prayer

Prayer:

We do not know what exists beyond this life, but Christians believe that those who die are held in God's love. Affirm that, if you can, by sharing in this prayer:

WE THANK YOU GOD FOR N,
WHOSE LIFE WE HAVE SHARED.

WE COMMEND *HIM/HER* TO YOU.
ENFOLD *HIM/HER* IN YOUR LOVE,
KEEP *HIM/HER* IN YOUR CARE,
NOW AND ALWAYS.
AMEN

If the committal is not to take place immediately, this blessing, or another, may be said:

Travel with us, God,
as we go together from this place.

Walk with us always,
and wherever we go we ask
that you never leave us or forsake us.

The committal:

Let us pray:

In the pain and joy of remembrance you have been with us, O God.
At this point of leaving stay with us still.

We have seen and known N and now we hand *him/her* back to you.
You created *him/her*.
As we lay *his/her* body to rest, receive *him/her* as your own.
Amen

And now let us pray for each other:

Parent God, you cry with us:
you understand what it feels like to be lost and forsaken.
Help us, as you understand our needs.
And as we are comforted, help us to comfort one another.
One day, if not now, may we be able to affirm that as we grieved,
even at the lowest point,
we were not separated from your love,
for we found it in neighbour and friend, sister and brother, parent and child.
And may that love surround us and bless us,
protect us and strengthen us.

Blessing:

The peace of God,
which is beyond our understanding,
keep us always in the love of God.
And the blessing of the Creator,
the compassion of Jesus
and the comfort of the Holy Spirit
remain with us and with those we love,
both living and dead,
this day and for evermore.
Amen

Andrew Pratt

Over

We walked in the graveyard.
The grave was open
waiting for the wooden box to come.
We snowballed each other to keep warm.
It was OK.
You would have laughed too.
And the cars came
and the flowers came
and the people.
And we laid you,
you and your ninety-one years of life,
in the grave.
And it was over.
And it was good.

Ruth Burgess

Children at funerals

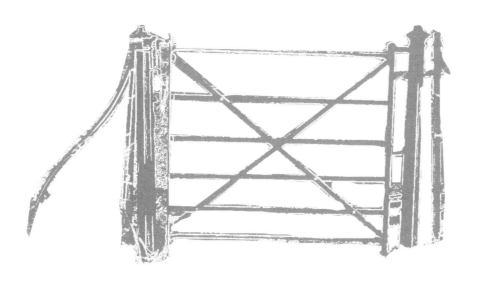

Children at funerals

Someone recently said to me: 'Funerals are designed for adults.' Given that children were not encouraged to attend funerals in Britain over past centuries, this is perhaps not a surprising comment.

With the current movement towards families having greater involvement in the planning of funeral services, a number of resources have been published. With the creation of groups and organisations focussing on the need to support young children and teenagers through the grief process, the discussion has widened to include practical activities that enable families to openly talk about grief and death.

Every child and every family is different. A decision about whether or not the child should attend all or some of the funeral is for the child and the family to decide, possibly in discussion with whoever is leading the service/ceremony.

What follows are tried and tested suggestions for practical activities that can include children, before, during and after a funeral, and a few suggestions for words that might work.

Before a funeral

- Talk with the child about death. Try to ensure that the child understands the concept of death – that a body has stopped working and that it doesn't feel pain or get lonely, or need food or air. Talk about burying a coffin or cremating a body.

- Create a memory box that contains items that provide good memories of the person: photos, a stone from a favourite place, a storybook that the child read with the person who has died, perfume, jewellery, a letter from the person who has died. This activity can begin before a person has died, and also take place in the weeks and months following a death, providing a focus for discussion, grieving, remembering.

- Create a memory book of photos of places and people that link the child with the person who has died. Let the child write about the photos.

- Let the child choose something to put into the coffin. Check with the undertaker about what is allowable.

- If the person is being buried/cremated in a cardboard coffin, the empty coffin could be at home and family and friends could get together and decorate it: paint, collage, fingerpaint …

- Take children to gather flower petals or leaves in a garden before the funeral: these can be sprinkled into the grave at the committal or on the coffin at the crematorium.

One family collected pinecones in the autumn – these bounce.

- Talk about the funeral with children and explain what will happen. Discuss with them how they could be involved. Give them the option of not attending the funeral or attending part of it. Make sure they have the possibility of leaving if they need to on the day. Have an adult known to them prepared to take them out if they want to leave.

- Talk about crying, and let children know that adults may cry at the funeral. Talk about crying that helps people feel better. Also let them know that people may laugh at something that is said, and that at a meal after the funeral it may be OK to play with friends and family.

- Involve children in writing the death notice/obituary for the newspaper or Internet.

- Involve children in designing the order of service for the funeral.

- Involve children in choosing readings, prayers, songs, music for the funeral …

- Involve children in planning a meal after the service.

- Ask whoever is leading the service to mention the children by name (or you may choose not to do this, depending on the child's needs).

If a child chooses not to attend a funeral

- Take photographs on the day so that you can make a memory book for them after the event.

- Video or record the funeral so that the child can watch it/listen to it, if they choose to, when they are older. (Some families find this helpful, others intrusive.)

- Take a drawing or a poem or a card from the child to put on the coffin.

- Tell them about the funeral later in the day.

- Take some flowers home from the funeral and use them as a focus for talking to the child about the funeral, and maybe say a prayer together for the person.

- Give them a way of saying goodbye: writing a card or prayer … making a drawing … lighting a candle … planting a seed … writing a message on a paper boat and letting it go downstream (try this out first to ensure the boat will float), letting go an eco-sky-lantern …

- Take them to visit the grave or involve them in burying/scattering the ashes.

At the funeral

If children are taking part in the service, let them see the building beforehand and practise what they are going to say or do.

Help them to follow/understand the order of the service.

Children can read things and do things together with other children and adults, e.g. at a funeral of an older person a group of grandchildren might read together from the Bible, or say a prayer, or sing a song …

Other involvement might include:

- reading something they have written

- reading something someone else has written

- reading a poem or a prayer

- playing some music

- lighting a candle

- putting a card on the coffin

- putting a photo or another object on the coffin

- draping the coffin in a cloth or a blanket (family activity)

- putting a flower or petals or leaves on the coffin. In winter this could be pinecones and fir branches.

Most funeral songs are written for adults, so if there is a song that the children involved know and understand it would be good to include it. Also, a song with a simple repetitive chorus might be appropriately included.

The spoken ministry and silence of a Quaker Meeting for Worship for a Funeral can be a healing experience for children who are familiar with silence. Shorter periods of silence within a funeral can balance the songs and words.

It might be appropriate to include a story or poem about death and grieving at the funeral that children can understand.

Funeral words that children can understand

Read through the service with the child before the funeral, discussing words that they don't understand. The pieces that follow were written with children in mind.

You (for the death of a family member)

You were our brother *(sister, mum, auntie …).*
You were special to us.
N, we love you.*

You shared our life.
You belong in our family.
N, we love you.

We will tell stories about you.
We will be sad. We will smile. We will miss you.
N, we love you.

We are saying goodbye to you today
but we will never forget you.
N, we love you.

* Could be said responsively

We are sad

We are sad today.
It's OK to be sad.
N has died and we miss him.
N was special to us:
he made us laugh and cry
and we love him.

We are saying goodbye today.
We won't see N again
but we won't forget him.

We are sad today.
We won't be always sad.
It will be OK to laugh tomorrow.

God bless (on the day of a funeral)

God bless N.
We ask you to look after her,
to keep her safe.
God bless us.
We ask you to look after us,
to listen to our prayers.

God bless today.
Help us to live in it.
Help us to love each other.

God bless N and us and everyone
and God bless tomorrow.
God, keep us all close to you.

At the graveside or outside the crematorium

- The child could release a balloon with a message tied to it: from them to the person who has died – everyone could do this.

- Summer funeral options might include releasing butterflies or doves.

- Sprinkle seeds or plant bulbs

- Before the funeral, take the child to gather rose petals in their garden, and then together sprinkle the petals onto the grave at the committal.

- The child might help the family fill in the grave, if they choose to.

After the funeral

- Look at memory boxes/books together.

- Talk about the person who has died.

- Create some kind of memorial to the person: a headstone, a bench … Somewhere that can be visited when appropriate.

- Plant bulbs indoors in bowls and observe the pattern of death and resurrection. Later replant the bulbs outside.

- If ashes are to be scattered involve the child in planning the ceremony.

- Mark special anniversaries: birthdays, Mother's Day, Father's Day, the anniversary of a death …

- Create a ritual to remember the person; something the child and the person liked doing: going for a meal … flying a kite … lighting a bonfire … planting carrots …

- Write a letter to the person who has died.

Helping children to write to or about the person who has died

- Talk about what the person looked like.

- Talk about the things they remember doing with the person … use photos as prompts … Make a list.

- Talk about what the person liked and disliked: food, clothes, getting up in the morning … Make a list.

- Talk about what made the person happy or sad.

- Talk about what was important to the person.

- Ask the child: 'If you had to tell a stranger what he/she was like, what would you say?'

- Ask the child: 'If the person was sitting next to you, what would you want to tell them about your day, your week … how you feel about them not being here?'

- Ask: 'What do you want to send the person?' … Kisses, a picture, hugs …?

Use thoughts and memories to write a poem:

N was special.
N was small and wore a red coat and a stripy scarf.
N loved strawberries – and hated cabbage.
N loved walking by the river and watching the ducks.
N read me stories at bedtime.
N loved music. It made her happy.
When her dog got hurt N was sad.
N loved her house and her garden. She fed the birds.
N and me shouted sometimes but we were good friends.
N was special.

N, I had a good day today. I had an egg and toast for breakfast. I went to school. Tonight I thought about you when we read the story you used to read me. Night, N. I love you.

Writing by children about those who have died:

My diary

Yesterday we went to my baby sister's grave. We took flowers and put them on the grass. It was sad. Me and Philip and Mum and Gemma all cried. We went and had an ice cream and then we went home.

– Tony, aged 7

Remember

Remember, remember where you are.
Remember, remember to tell us.
Remember, remember that you will be with me.
I remember when you were alive,
I remember when we played.
I remember when we would skateboard,
I remember when we played sticky in the mud.

I shall always remember us going to Boyne Park.
I shall always remember the sadness.
You made me laugh and laugh and laugh.

– Debra Mullaly, aged 13, remembering a sister who died in a road accident.

Teenagers

There are websites that teenagers may find helpful: e.g. Graffiti walls, Skyscape of memories (see Winston's Wish website: www.winstonswish.org.uk).

Teenagers could:

• be involved in creating the funeral service.

• share in making the meal after the funeral.

• design the order of service.

- read, play an instrument, light a candle at the funeral.

- sit with their friends at the funeral.

There are a number of stories that explore death and grieving that teenagers might find helpful: see Helpful websites and books (p205).

Listening and exploring

Children have an awareness of death and their understanding of its finality grows with experience. When talking to children about death and funerals, listen to the children's questions and let their questions lead the conversation. Conversations may be very short. They will often be returned to and repeated. Care needs to be taken with the language and concepts used: 'We've lost grandma' could mean one thing to an adult and something entirely different to a child. Also, children's questions can come at any time and from anywhere and a short honest answer may be more appropriate than a long discussion.

A conversation

'Who's buried there?'
a three-year-old voice
asked from the back of the tombstone.
'Sharon's little girl,' I said,
digging into the sunken grass and turning it over.
'Why is she dead?' he asked.
'Somebody hurt her,' I answered.
'Like somebody punched and kicked her?'
'Yes,' I said.
'I don't kick my friends at nursery,' he replied.

'I might get a spade for Christmas,' he said,
eyeing mine up for size.
'You might,' I answered.
'What's it for?' he said,
pointing to the new turf
as I measured it along the grave.
'Like a blanket,' I suggested.
'To keep her warm?'
'To keep her warm,' I agreed.

'I'm not dead,' he said.
'No – you're alive,' I told him.
'What's alive?' he said.
'You can walk and shout and see … and talk,' I said.
(You can also ask hundreds of three-year-old questions
that are making me smile,
I thought – but I didn't tell him.)

I slapped the turf down and we poured
the water into it,
watching it bubble and disappear.
Beginning to tidy up
I poured out
some stale water from the vases.
'That's water that smells,' he said.
I agreed.

Then together we examined three dead slugs
that had drowned
and now lay bloated on the new grass.
'You'll have to clear them away,' he said,
and I did.

Ruth Burgess

Sentences and blessings for funerals

Biblical sentences for funerals

God is your shelter.
God's arms are underneath you forever.
Deuteronomy 33:27a

This is how much God loved the world.
He sent Jesus.
And whoever trusts in Jesus will always be alive.
John 3:16

God is not against us.
God is for us
and nothing
in life or death
can separate us from God's love.
Romans 8:31a,38f

Blessed are those who mourn.
They will be comforted.
Matthew 5:4

God's love and mercy goes on forever,
fresh as the morning,
sure as the rising sun.
God is everything to me.
I put my hope in God.
Lamentations 3:22–24

Nobody has ever heard or seen
what God has prepared
for those who love Him.
1 Corinthians 2:9

Christians believe that Jesus died and rose again.
So it will be for followers of Jesus.
God will give them life like Jesus.
Thessalonians 4:14,17

Always, we will be with God.
1 Thessalonians 4:17

All my life God has loved me.
I will live in God's house forever.

Psalm 23

In the beginning God.
In the end God.
God's words are true and can be trusted.

Revelations 21:5f

God says:
Don't be afraid.
I love you.
I honour you.
You are precious to me.
I will always be with you.
I will bring you home.

Isaiah 43:1ff

Jesus said
I will be with you
to the end of time.

Matthew 28:20

Give thanks:
God is good.
God's love goes on forever.

Psalm 136:1

God will wipe away
the tears from your eyes.

Revelation 21:4a

God is everywhere.
God is in the world of the dead and the living.

Psalm 139:8

I will always be beside you.
I will never abandon you.

Joshua 1:5b

There is a time to weep
and a time to laugh,
a time to mourn
and a time to dance,
a time to be born
and a time to die.
Ecclesiastes 3:2–4

God is our shelter and strength.
God is always ready to help
in times of trouble.
Psalm 46:1

Trust God.
Tell God your troubles.
God listens.
God is our refuge.
Psalm 62:8

You, God, have always been our home.
You were eternally God.
You will be God forever.
Psalm 90:1

God, your love goes on forever.
Complete in us
the work that you have begun.
Psalm 138:8

Jesus said:
'Come to me all of you who are weary,
all of you whose load is heavy,
and I will give you rest.'
Matthew 11:28

What we see now
is like a dim reflection
in a mirror.

One day
we will see face to face.
What we know now
is only part of what there is to know.
One day
we will know God
as God already knows and loves us.

1 Corinthians 13:12

Ruth Burgess

Sentences and blessings based on prayers from the Carmina Gadelica

You are going home today to your home of winter,
to your home of autumn, of spring and summer.
You are going home to your home forever.

Sleep tonight in the arms of Mary.
Sleep tonight in the hug of Jesus.
Sleep tonight in the kiss of God.

May the God of love surround you.
May the strength of Jesus protect you.
May the Holy Spirit seek you and find you and bring you home.

May God who brought you into the light of each morning
bring you today into the light of eternity.

We are placing your soul and your body
into the love and life of God.

We give you into the safe charge of the angels,
sacred, strong and steadfast.
We give you into the safe charge of the angels,
who will follow the guiding stars
and bring you home to God.

Through life
through death
be the herding of God about your feet.
Safe and whole may you reach home.

Walk this day with God.
Walk this day with Jesus.
Walk this day with the Holy Spirit.
Walk in love and justice with the three all-kindly.

Watch over me
each evening.
Watch with me
each morning.
Watch me always
and allure me home.

As you were at our life's beginning
so be with us at our journey's close.

The sun of the heavens.
The moon of the skies.
The stars
and the path of the wanderers.
The sand,
the stones
and the dry shore
be yours today and forever.

With all the tears of your loving
with all the laughter of your living
with all the questions of your journey
go now into the wonder of life eternal.

May your guardian angel come to meet you.
May you be shepherded in the fold of the saints.
May you be led to the court of Christ.

Today, tonight, forever
may you be at home in heaven.

God in our darkness,
shield us this night and every night,
till light and dawn shall come.

The joyful smile of God be yours
on the sunny day of your salvation.

The light of the sun,
each day that dawns,
each new beginning
is the face of the God of life.

Christ be your peace
at your ingathering
and may Michael kindly,
high king of all the holy angels,
take possession of your beloved soul
and shield it home.

Give O God
strong love
the joy of forgiveness
the soul's healing
the home of salvation
and the hospitality of bright peace.

Jesus has his arms around you
Mary kisses you to sleep
Sleep this night in the love of all loves
Sleep, O beloved, in the God of life.

May the God of life
be at peace with you
be your smooth way
be your guiding star.

May the God of life
be at peace with you
from your lying down
to your rising anew.

The grace of God be with us
the love of Christ be with us
the kindness of the Spirit be with us
for an hour
for ever
for eternity.

Ruth Burgess

Bits and pieces for funerals

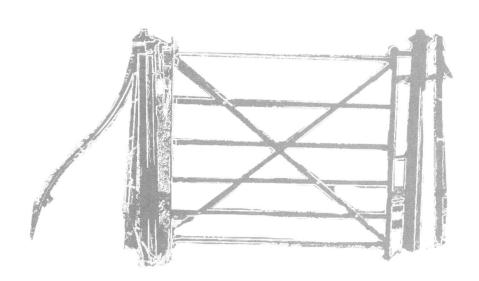

We are here today

Adapt as necessary

We are here today to say goodbye to N:
to give thanks for her life
to remember her story
and to stand with her
in the cycle of birth and death and resurrection
where she and we belong.

We are here today in a church:
for some of us this is a familiar place,
for some of us this is a strange place.
We are here today in a place
where people have always prayed to and questioned God.

We are here today in a crematorium;
this place has seen tears and smiles, sadness and questions.
This is a place where we can say goodbye to N
in ways that will make sense for us today and tomorrow.

We are here today in the open air,
in the midst of seeds and leaves,
of pollen and dust.
We are here in the midst of a world that
turns through time
and changes
and ages
and is continually reborn.

We are here today in N's home,
a place that is familiar to her
and to most of us.
This is the last time we will
be together with N in this place.
This is a good place to remember
and say goodbye to N.
And although she is here
in her body
and in our memories,
she is ready to leave us
to carry on her journey into death and life.

And we are glad to be here
to send her on her way.

Ruth Burgess

This is the place

This is the place
where death meets life,
where sorrow is present,
where hard questions are asked
and not always answered.

This is the place
where pain is felt,
where partings are made real,
where holy words
can ring empty and hollow.

This is the place
where we ask 'Why?',
where we cry 'What now?'
Where God is near
or feels so far away.

This is the place
where emotions are mixed,
where tears are shed,
where memories return
of brighter yesterdays.

This is the place
where God says, 'I know.'
Where God says, 'I am here.'
Where God sheds a tear
along with us.

This is the place
where God understands,
where God stands and waits,
where Jesus says
'I went through it.'

This is the place
where Easter is hope,
where eternity is God,
where each ending
becomes a beginning.

This is the place
where God is all around
and very much alive
because we need him
here in this place.

Marjorie Dobson

We're here because

Adapt as necessary

We're here because of God.
We're here because God gave us N to learn from and to love.

God brought N to birth,
held her hand while she learned to walk,
let her fall down and get up all on her own,
set her on her path and was with her all the way –
when she danced and when she limped.
God brought N to death and she died in God's arms.

We're here because of God.
We're here because God gave us N
to learn from and to love.

Sally Foster-Fulton

This is your time

Adapt as necessary

This is your time …
He held your hand
and your heart in his.
You gave him his centre – gave him his foundation
and helped him to fly.

This is your time …
You who loved him and lived with him,
knew him inside out,
smiled at his habits
and weren't above rolling your eyes on occasion:
you were his and he was yours.

This is your time …
to sit with his spirit,
to hold on to each other,
to take time to gather yourselves
and gather him up
into your hearts and memories.

This is your time
to say goodbye …

Sally Foster-Fulton

Prayer of approach at a funeral

Shepherd God,
creating for us the green pastures
and the quiet waters of this planet
for us to walk in and to take our rest:
we thank and praise you
for all the blessings of this world
and of the life you have given to each one of us.

Jesus our companion,
walking with us all the way,
leading us into right relationships
of friendship and love, and staying with us
even in the midst of sin and death:
we thank and praise you
for your strong, enduring love,
a great comfort – and so much more.

Spirit of Life and Love,
feeding our lives with your very self,
and assuring us of the truth
of the mystery of eternal life,

beginning now:
we thank and praise you
for your nourishing, anointing presence,
never far from our side.

Triune God,
dancing around us,
among us and within,
be present to us now, we pray,
and help us to worship you, and to trust you,
as we seek again the forgiveness of our sins,
the certainty of resurrection,
and the assurance of the victory
of life and love over the power of death and the grave.

We ask this in the name
of Jesus Christ our Lord.

John Harvey

We are here with lots of questions

We are here with lots of questions.
No one knows what happens to us after death.
We know that our bodies age and die.
We know that our bones and dust are part of the cycle of death and life.
Some of us believe that God is part of who we are
and that God's love and our love will go on forever.
Some of us recognise that we live on in the memories of those who know us.
Some of us see that the cycle of death and life and resurrection
happens to seeds and animals,
to plants and human beings –
we are all caught up in it together.

We are here with lots of questions.
It is safe to ask them.
It is right to live with them.
Death and life and resurrection are part of who we are.

Ruth Burgess

God says to us in Jesus

God says to us in Jesus:
I love you.
I will always love you.
My love is stronger than death.

Some days we seem to want more than that.

We want to know what happens to us when we die.
We want to know if we will meet our loved ones again.
We want to know if there's a place or a state called heaven,
and what it's like.
We want to know if we'll meet Jesus.
We want to know if part of us lives on forever.
And we want answers now, before we die.

And God says to us in Jesus:
There's no way I can explain it to you now.
You'll have to wait and see.
But I've been there and I will be with you.
I will always love you.
My love is stronger than death.

Ruth Burgess

Goodbye and God bless you

It is time to say
Goodbye N.
Goodbye and God bless you.
SAFE JOURNEY HOME.

Goodbye N.
We have prayed for you.*
We have told your story.
Goodbye and God bless you.
SAFE JOURNEY HOME.

Goodbye N.
We want you to know
that we love you and miss you.
Goodbye and God bless you.
SAFE JOURNEY HOME.

Goodbye N.
Go well on your journey.
Goodbye and God bless you.
SAFE JOURNEY HOME.

* Or 'read poems/sang songs for you …'

Ruth Burgess

Go now

Go now
Go and be one
with the winds and the stars
and the warmth of the sun
Go in peace
GO IN LOVE

Go now
Go and be one
with the seeds and the trees
and the flowers that blossom
Go in peace
GO IN LOVE

Go now
Go with your hopes
with your wonder
with your questions
Go in peace
GO IN LOVE

Go now
Go and be one
with all that is
and all that will be.
Go in peace
GO IN LOVE

Ruth Burgess

A journey blessing (Psalm 121)

God bless you
God shelter you
God keep you from evil.

God bless you
God help you
God shelter your soul.

God bless you
God lead you
in your comings and goings.

God bless you
God guard you
on your journey safe home.

Ruth Burgess

I am with you (Matthew 28:20)

Listen to what Jesus told us:

Jesus said:
I am with you
in your end and your beginning.
I am always at your side.

Jesus said:
I am with you
today and tomorrow.
I am always at your side.

Jesus said:
I am with you
in your smiles and your sorrow.
I am always at your side.

Jesus said:
I am with you
until this world is over.
I am always at your side.

Ruth Burgess

What can separate us from the love of God in Christ Jesus? (Romans 8)

What can separate us from the love of God in Christ Jesus?

Shall pain?
No
Shall despair?
No
Shall time?
No
Shall tears?
No
Shall evil?
No
Shall peril?
No
Shall life?
No
Shall death?
No
Shall things to come?
No

What can separate us from the love of God in Christ Jesus?

Only one answer.
One answer forever:

Nothing can separate us from the love of God.

Ruth Burgess

Deep in the earth

Deep in the earth
we lay you down
WE LAY YOU DOWN WITH LOVE

Deep in our hearts
we lay you down
WE LAY YOU DOWN WITH LOVE

Deep in God's peace
we lay you down
WE LAY YOU DOWN WITH LOVE

Ruth Burgess

We wrap you round

We wrap you round
with earth and flowers
WE WRAP YOU ROUND WITH LOVE

We wrap you round
with songs and stories
WE WRAP YOU ROUND WITH LOVE

We wrap you round
with prayers for your journey
WE WRAP YOU ROUND WITH LOVE

Ruth Burgess

In the land

You were born here
You grew up here
You belong here
WE LAY YOU DOWN IN THE LAND

With your tears
With your laughter
With your story
WE LAY YOU DOWN IN THE LAND

With your friends
With your family
With your community
WE LAY YOU DOWN IN THE LAND

With love and completeness
With hope and faithfulness
(person's full name)
WE LAY YOU DOWN IN THE LAND

Ruth Burgess

Responses for a burial

Into the darkness
and warmth of the earth
WE LAY YOU DOWN

Into the sadness
and smiles of our memories
WE LAY YOU DOWN

Into the cycle of living and dying
and rising again
WE LAY YOU DOWN

May you rest in peace,
in fulfilment, in loving
MAY YOU RUN STRAIGHT HOME
INTO GOD'S EMBRACE

Ruth Burgess

Responses for a cremation

Into the freedom of wind and sunshine
WE LET YOU GO

Into the dance of the stars and the planets
WE LET YOU GO

Into the wind's breath and the hands of the Star-maker
WE LET YOU GO

We love you, we miss you, we want you to be happy
GO SAFELY, GO DANCING, GO RUNNING HOME

Ruth Burgess

Ashes

Scattering dad's ashes

The lady vicar, in full ecclesiastical vestments,
strode across the ploughed field, prayer book in hand.
My wife stumbled along behind, supporting her mother.
I brought up the rear, entrusted with carrying the urn.

We arrived at the edge.
'This is the spot,' said mum.
'This is where the family ashes are traditionally scattered
over the edge of the cliff.'
To me it looked like every spot on the clifftop,
for a distance of at least half a mile in both directions.

The vicar read some prayers and scripture verses,
and we prepared to scatter the ashes.

'If I were you,' the vicar said quietly,
'I'd crouch down and drop handfuls over the edge.
If you stand up and throw them
they tend to blow back in your face.'

I thought *You've done this before.*

Or was it an optional module at theological college:
'Practical management of scattering ashes',
along with 'Recent developments in the study of Ecclesiastes'
and 'How to counsel those affected by a World Cup defeat'?

Or did the church warden have a quiet word when the vicar arrived?
'In a seaside parish like this we do get those
who want to scatter their loved one's ashes over the clifftop and ...'

Brian Ford

Non-burial at sea

My father never set much store by death.
In hindsight, knowing that, perhaps we should have buried him.
Instead we took the easy option, and we burnt him to ash.

We scattered parts of him in various places,
making it hard to reassemble, if the thought ever tempted him,
but we took the last plastic container to Columba's Bay.

We clambered out beyond the saintly metamorphic stones
and found a place where rock dropped sheer into deep water.
There we upended the container with the last residue of beard and bones.

This was well witnessed. Meeting that beloved sea,
the ash took shape – a circle ten feet in diameter;
a smoothness, where the sky reflected differently.

It hung still for a few minutes. Then it set out on a journey,
rippling out, unhurried, to the isles in the far West.
We stood and watched it for as long as we could see.

We should have known. Where else would he have gone?
How foolish to presume he could be laid to rest.
And if the ash dispersed, look how the image shimmers on.

Roddy Cowie

Scattered

Scattered
to the four winds dancing
to the deep seas rolling
to the ends of the earth.

Let loose
into the seasons turning
into nights and mornings
into the vault of time.

Gathered
into our thoughts and memories
into our family story
into the history of our world.

Living
in the small seeds growing
in the settling stardust
in the heart of God.

Ruth Burgess

Into the air

Into the air
Into everywhere
WE LET YOU GO

Into the rain's dance
Into the wind's strength
WE LET YOU GO

Into the sunlight
Into the starlight
WE LET YOU GO

Go with our love
Go with our wonder
GO AND BE ONE
WITH ALL THAT IS

Ruth Burgess

Into the earth

Into the earth,
seeds mingling with ashes,
WE DIG YOU DEEP.

Into our memories,
smiles mingling with sadness,
WE DIG YOU DEEP.

Into our story,
laughter mingling with wonder,
WE DIG YOU DEEP.

Into the earth,
death mingling with resurrection,
WE DIG YOU DEEP.

When the flowers grow
and the sun dances
WE WILL REMEMBER YOU WITH LOVE.

Ruth Burgess

As we walk*

As we walk,
seeds and ashes
we let you go.

Along the hedgerows
beside the pathway
we let you go.

Onto the grass
among the daisies
we let you go.

Under the trees
in dappled sunlight
we let you go.

Into the air
where the winds take you
we let you go.

Onto the earth
dug over and waiting
we let you go.

Into the rhythm
of weather and seasons
we let you go.

When the flowers bloom
and the sun warms us
we will remember you with love.

Ruth Burgess

* To be used when scattering seeds with ashes.
  Choose appropriate stanzas.

Into water

Into the running water
into the journey to the sea*
WE LET YOU GO

Into the dance of the river
into the dance of the tides
WE LET YOU GO

Into the glory of God
into the wonder of creation
WE LET YOU GO

May the God who cradled the oceans,
the Son who went fishing
and the Spirit who danced on the waters
receive you kindly,
with joy and with love.
AMEN

Ruth Burgess

* If ashes are put into the sea use 'Into the dance of the waves,
  into the roll of the sea …'

Ashes to stardust

Dust
Stardust
Living we are part of it,
dying we are one with it:
Ashes to stardust
WE LET YOU GO

Dust
Stardust
Dancing in the atmosphere,
whirling through the universe:
Ashes to stardust
WE LET YOU GO

Dust
Stardust
Living in our memories,
smiling in our storytelling:
Ashes to stardust
WE LET YOU GO

Dust
Stardust
Into here and now
and everywhere and forever:
Ashes to stardust
WE LET YOU GO

Dust
Stardust
With our journey prayers,
with our love and blessing:
Ashes to stardust
WE LET YOU GO

Ruth Burgess

The communion of saints

I used to scatter ashes of people on the green land of Iona
and sometimes the whirling wind, altering direction,
would blow them back on me, and dust clung to my clothes,
my skin, my hair.
But I did not mind.
Their dust is mine, and mine theirs.
I, we, they, all of us,
partake of one another's dust,
change,
exchange,
are incorporated.

And my grandmother,
and William Shakespeare,
and Brian, lying near John Smith on Iona,

and John Smith too,
and Columba, and the black slave who said,
Ain't I a woman?,
and the man who said, This time together
will always be a part of me,
and the woman who is where I am not for me,
and I for her,
and children and women and men
are all a part of me
and I of them,
incorporated,
in communion,
speaking, moving, living
in each other,
breathing in each other
on and on and on.

I give great thanks.

Kathy Galloway

Ashes on the beach

Ashes on the beach.
We write your name.
We build a sand boat.
We miss you.
WE LOVE YOU.

Ashes on the beach.
We picnic.
We sit and tell stories.
We miss you.
WE LOVE YOU.

Ashes on the beach.
The tide is turning.
The tide is running.
We miss you.
WE LOVE YOU.

Ashes on the beach.
We let you go into the ocean.
We let you go with our blessing.
We let you go in love.
AMEN

Ruth Burgess

Turning the ashes

*In some cemeteries, gardens of remembrance and graveyards ashes are scattered
in a specific area of ground. This is a liturgy to accompany an annual event where
the ashes scattered throughout a year are turned into the earth.*

Opening responses:

Ashes to ashes, dust to dust:
FROM GOD WE CAME
TO GOD WE RETURN

In God we live, in God we have our being:
FROM GOD WE CAME
TO GOD WE RETURN

We are part of a cycle of living and dying:
FROM GOD WE CAME
TO GOD WE RETURN

In God we die, in God we go on living:
FROM GOD WE CAME
TO GOD WE RETURN

Words to be said as the earth is turned:

Matter to matter
ashes to ashes
dust to dust
WE TURN THIS EARTH

Diggers and burrowers
gardeners and growers

ploughers and furrowers
WE TURN THIS EARTH

Spring to summer
summer to harvest
harvest to hibernation
WE TURN THIS EARTH

Turn us God
turn us with the seasons
turn us with the generations
TURN US WITH THE EARTH.

Words of remembrance: *(to be said after people have had the opportunity to think and talk about those who have died)*

For those we remember
for those who lie here
THANKS BE TO GOD

For those we know
for travellers and strangers
THANKS BE TO GOD

For all our stories
for all our memories
THANKS BE TO GOD

For the love that surrounds them
for the love that sustains us
THANKS BE TO GOD

Closing responses:

We travel on
from birth to dying
WE ARE TRAVELLING HOME

We travel on
from dying to living
WE ARE TRAVELLING HOME

We travel on
through pain and laughter
WE ARE TRAVELLING HOME

We travel on
with hope and wonder
WE ARE TRAVELLING HOME TO GOD.

Bible readings: *John 12:24; Genesis 3:19; Ecclesiastes 3:1–8; Psalm 90:1,6,12,14,16,17; Psalm 103:13–18*

Songs: 'When we are living, we are in the Lord', by Roberto Escamilla and John L. Bell (CH4); 'Dust, dust and ashes' (traditional)

Ruth Burgess

High on the hills

High on the hills
where the rocks
meet the sky
we leave you.

Where the winds blow
and the sun dances
we leave you.

Where the birds soar
and the moon shines
we leave you.

We leave you
where you loved to climb.

We leave you safe
beneath the stars.

Ruth Burgess

Here where you belong

You used to walk here,
you loved the noise and the bustle,
you loved the buses and the shops.

You used to talk here,
with your family and your neighbours,
with strangers on the street and with friends.

You used to watch here,
for new flowers along the pathways,
for stalking cats and wary birds.

In our memories you are still here,
in our tears and in our laughter,
in our stories and our hugs.

So we have come to put your ashes here,
here where you walked and talked and wondered,
here in your neighbourhood,
here where you belong.

Ruth Burgess

Elemental

When my time is over
and fire has consumed
all flesh, take my dust
and scatter it
where you can feel
earth, water, rushing air
that I may be
whole.

Then take away with you
memories, burning in fire,
fresh as air, rolling as sea,
still as the earth
and this shall be
my resurrection.

Joy Mead

Stones and memorials

Prayer at the dedication of Craig's bench, MacLeod Centre, Iona *

Loving God, watching over the world,
seeing the smallest sparrow fall,
we thank you for the life of Craig,
a fragile human being worth everything to you.

We thank you for his watchfulness, his listening,
his awareness of your world,
his enjoyment of Iona and of life in community;
for the way he made us more aware
and encouraged us to care.

God-with-us, who sits down by our side,
thank you for being there for Craig's family,
giving anger when it was needed
and joy, courage and strength to go on.
Thank you for being there for Craig and in Craig,
helping us to see that God is in everyone.

And may all who sit on this bench and read Craig's name
reflect on the beauty of Iona,
rejoice in the company of other human beings,
and remember that wherever we are,
and whoever we are, you are with us.
Amen

Jan Sutch Pickard

* Craig Whinnett was an Associate member of the Iona Community.

Creator God, hear us

John Ellerton, who composed the hymn 'The day Thou gavest', was Vicar of St Michael and All Angels Church, Crewe Green from 1860–1872. It is said that he sat on the vestry steps and composed that favourite hymn at the end of a busy day. The following prayers were written for a weekend when his work was remembered, but they could be adapted for any occasion when it is appropriate to pray and give thanks for those with creative gifts.

Prayers:

As we give thanks for the life and work of John Ellerton* in this place,
we pray for all composers, musicians, songwriters and artists …
Lord hear us:
CREATOR GOD, HEAR US.

We pray for theologians and poets, for storytellers and preachers …
Lord hear us:
CREATOR GOD, HEAR US.

We pray for those who use their creative gifts in horticulture and agriculture,
in caring for the earth …
Lord hear us:
CREATOR GOD, HEAR US.

We pray for those whose skills have led to advancement in science and medicine:
for researchers and doctors, for surgeons and nurses …
Lord hear us:
CREATOR GOD, HEAR US.

Lastly, we pray that we may develop and use our skills
to share in God's work of creation.
Lord hear us:
CREATOR GOD, HEAR US.
AMEN

S. Anne Lawson

* The name of any other local writer, artist or creative person could be inserted here.

Planting of memorial trees

God of young plants and tiny creatures,
bless these trees
with summer rain and winter sun,
that they may grow strong enough
for the birds to come
and nest in their branches.

God of beauty and wonder,
bless these trees
with autumn winds and spring rainbows,
that they may grow tall enough
for us to come
and stand in their shade.

God of our lives and memories,
bless these trees
and bless us
as we remember _____.
Be our delight, our strength, our comforter,
all the moments
of our nights and days.

Ruth Burgess

Snowdrops

I love to see snowdrops flowering in my garden – they are a sign that spring is on its way. My snowdrops are very special to me for another reason. They came from my grandmother's garden in the village where I was born. Late one spring I visited her and, as we often did, we talked about gardening and plants. When she heard that we had no snowdrops in our garden she insisted we took some from her own garden's large clump of bulbs. My grandmother died a few weeks later. I think of my grandmother when the snowdrops flower each year.

I have now moved several times since she gave me those plants, but each time I have taken with me some bulbs from that original clump and planted them in our garden. They remind me of my grandmother's love of flowers and the way she stimulated my own interest in gardening. They remind me of her generosity, her willingness to share what gave her pleasure and her love for me. Although the memories evoked by my snowdrops are tinged with sadness, they are also joyful.

Memories are one of the most precious gifts God has given us. At a funeral I often encourage those present to cherish their memories, as they will be a continuing source of comfort to them. Our treasured memories of time together can help sustain us through difficult days and bring a smile of joyful recollection, even in the midst of deep pain.

There is another lesson we can learn from snowdrops. Their flowers and leaves soon die away and all that remains of them is a memory. However, in late winter the next year they return to life to bring us joy again. In John's Gospel Jesus says: *'I am the resurrection and the life. They who believe in me will live, even though they die; and whoever lives and believes in me will never die.'* Jesus gives us that wonderful assurance that those who trust in his power to give new life have the gift of eternal life, that death will not be the end for us, and we will be made alive again through him: God is greater than the power of death.

May we know joy in the memories of our loved ones
and peace in the face of death,
through trust in Jesus.

Simon Taylor

Gone

Your memorial stone
has been
washed clean
by the daily tide,
the ordinary rhythm
of life's ebb and flow.

My care in painting
the inscription
is not lost,
for all that matters comes
from the same source
and returns, if freely
let go.

Yvonne Morland

Memorial

There is no grave
on which to place
and replace flowers,
brightening a corner
with your memory.
No headstone keeps your name
permanent in chiselled marble.
No grassy mound
to weed or water
for conscience' sake,
or to fulfil
the local graveyard bye-laws.

It was a conscious choice
not to identify you
with a patch of earth.

For now you cannot be confined.
Your spirit soars,
free from pain,
in every breeze that blows.
Your soul is safe
with the God
whose existence
you denied and doubted,
or affirmed in faith
in testing stages on your road.

And we who knew you,
see you in the soaring birds,
the crashing waves,
the towering trees
you loved
and taught us to love.

Your memorial is your delight in life
that brightened our days
and cannot be forgotten.

Marjorie Dobson

This is your stone

N,
this is your stone
the marker of your life on earth.

N,
you are more than this stone:
you are laughter on our lips
and tears in our eyes
and love in our hearts

N,
we love you and miss you
and we *raise/place* this stone on your grave
to tell friends and strangers
that your *bones/ashes* lie here.

N,
this is your stone.
May it sing of our love for you
today and tomorrow
and into the coming years.

Ruth Burgess

Anniversaries and remembering

Still meeting you (for mum)

You are not gone.

Snowdrops
Stewed blackberry and apple
Cowslips
I am still meeting you.

Royal Doulton
Clean sheets
Blue Grass hand lotion
You are there beside me smiling.

Welsh cakes
The Lady
An afternoon at the seaside
I walk in your footsteps.

It's 12 years now.

We shared so much.
And we were so different.

And I am still meeting you.

Ruth Burgess

Last night I thought she was with me again

Last night,
just for a few moments,
I thought she was with me again.
Half asleep,
I thought I felt someone stirring in the bed beside me.
A confused moment of hope.
Then I remembered the hospice,
the memorial service,
the crematorium.
And waking, I realised
that the dog,
as lonely as I was,
had climbed on to the bed alongside me.

And I thanked God for small,
very small
comfort.

Brian Ford

Family bereavement

Family bereavement I

My uncle died, and left
a huge pile of money
and nothing else.

Family bereavement II

My uncles died, and left
photos of the two of them, inseparable,
a strong smell of fag smoke,
and barely enough to pay for the funerals.

Family bereavement III

My auntie died, and left
photos of kids and babies (not her own),
photos of priests and pilgrimages (she was devout),
photos of weddings and parties (not too devout),
dozens of pictures of Mary and Jesus (they were friends of hers),
drawers full of hankies and nice bars of soap
(kept for the sake of the person who gave them),
needles and string and pins in tins (thrift is a virtue),
clothes neatly folded and mended and washed (so is cleanliness),
a Z-bed for visitors (and hospitality),
seven address books and plenty of Christmas cards,
letters from family and friends far away,
envelopes with names on,
gifts for us all when she'd gone –

and enough for a ginormous party.

Catherine Harkin

Potatoes

Every year on Good Friday
my grandfather, God rest his soul,
would plant potatoes.
Spuds he called them.
Be it early or late
he marked the death of Christ
with a spade and a trench.
By Easter the soil had warmed,
frosts were past
and those fragile shoots
would be buried in the rich loam.

We're told the body of Jesus was
laid in a tomb under the earth
on that day long ago.
Then in secret
change took place.

Resurrection's busting new life continues.
From what looked dry
shrivelled and dead
sprout roots and leaves
continuing the everyday miracle
of the wondrous cycle of life.
Tubers bring forth tubers –
and a tenfold return is
almost guaranteed.

Grandpa loved his spuds;
never had lunch without them
and never ate without giving thanks.

John Butterfield

We re-member

For saying goodbye to friends

In the delights of the body,
in tastes and smells, in colours and senses,
WE RE-MEMBER YOU.

In the stories and laughter,
the gossip and secrets of friendship,
WE RE-MEMBER YOU.

In the risk of vulnerability,
the encouragement and the support,
WE RE-MEMBER YOU.

In the depths of our sharing,
the hopes and insights, the longings and dreams,
WE RE-MEMBER YOU.

In our bones, in our flesh and blood,
in our struggling, our playing, our living,
WE RE-MEMBER YOU.

Jan Berry

A year on

At 6:30pm,
exactly a year
after she died,
I looked at my watch
and thought
I've made it!
I've made it through the first year.
I thought today would be dreadful
but I kept myself busy
and, with your help, Lord,
I've done it.
People told me that the first year would be the worst,
and indeed, it was pretty grim at times,
but with your help, Lord,
I made it.
Thank you.

Brian Ford

A Mass for children who have died in pregnancy

Prayer:

For the times we have not turned to you in our need:
LORD HAVE MERCY.
For the times we have blamed ourselves or others unjustly:
CHRIST HAVE MERCY.
For the smallness of our faith:
LORD HAVE MERCY.

Merciful God,
hear our prayer and console us;
as we renew our faith in your Son,
whom you raised from the dead,
strengthen our hope that our departed children
will share in his resurrection.

Readings: *Isaiah 65:17–20, Psalm 84:1–2*

Gospel reading: Matthew 18:1–4,10

Repetition of baptismal vows:

We express our belief in the life of our children with Christ.

Standing together with them in the presence of God, and in the communion of saints, we repeat our baptismal vows … *(Vows are said)*

Bidding prayers:

We pray for the departed children of all here present,
that they may know the eternal love of their Creator.
We give them into God's arms and ask that they may also pray for us.
Lord hear us.
LORD GRACIOUSLY HEAR US.

We pray for all who wrongly blame themselves for the loss of a child,
that they may forgive themselves and be healed.
Lord hear us.
LORD GRACIOUSLY HEAR US.

We pray for all those who have hurt or angered us in our grief
by speaking or acting clumsily.
Lord hear us.
LORD GRACIOUSLY HEAR US.

Prayer over the gifts:

Lord we are united in this sacrament by the love of Jesus Christ.
Accept these gifts and receive your children into the glory of your Son,
who is Lord forever and ever.

Prayer after communion:

Lord, may this Eucharist we have shared
fill us with your courage and love.

Frances Blodwell, née Copsey

Hogmanay for Charlie

Year ending,
a time for looking back –
the ups and downs,
laughter and pain –
a time to celebrate and to forget.

Year ending,
a time for looking forward –
hopes and fears,
plans made –
a time to share and to change.

But also this:

Year ending,
a life ending,
a time for looking back –
the ups and downs,
laughter and pain –
shared years as one.

Year ending,
a time for looking forward –
empty lonely days,
decisions to be made –
a gathering of memories,
an easing of pain.

This year ending
offering the final farewell
to a dearly loved husband
and friend.

Katherine Rennie

I didn't go to her grave today

I didn't go to her grave today …

… and for the first time, I didn't feel guilty about that.
So much of my grief is wrapped up in myself,
almost as if I'm blaming her for leaving me.
Or, am I blaming God that she is gone?

But today, I didn't go to see her grave.
She is not there,
only her body – the shell of what she was –
still is, to me.
The shell I can let go in time.
The essence of her is around me here.
Is this what they call resurrection?

I didn't go to see her grave today,
but I thanked God
that I had shared my life with her.

Marjorie Dobson

Liturgy for the anniversary of a death

The setting for this liturgy is some kind of shared gathering: a family meal, a picnic, a meeting of friends … The liturgy is participative and the leadership should be shared. Take responsibility for each other's feelings. Laughter and tears are appropriate in this setting.

Opening responses:

Come among us God.
You cast the planets into space
and cradle the sparrow in her nest.
COME GOD AND MEET US HERE.

Come among us God.
You bless the poor and the broken
and stand by the sad and the strong.
COME GOD AND MEET US HERE.

Come among us God.
You dance in the silence

and shine in the darkness.
COME GOD AND MEET US HERE.

A song

Readings: Psalm 139:7–10, Revelation 21:3–4, John 14: 1–3

A space to remember:

An opportunity to remember those who have died – to tell stories, sing songs, share memories, photographs, silence, laughter and sadness …

You could use a ritual action: lighting a candle, placing a stone or a flower, floating petals in water, playing a game …

Words to close the time of remembering:

All our laughter, all our sadness
SAFE NOW IN GOD'S HANDS

All our anger, all our gladness
SAFE NOW IN GOD'S HANDS

All our stories, all our memories
SAFE NOW IN GOD'S HANDS

Those we remember, those we love
SAFE NOW IN GOD'S HANDS

A shared time:

Sing a song together, listen to music, share food and drink …

Closing responses:

We ask for the love of God
AND THE MESSAGES OF ANGELS

The laughter of Jesus
AND THE STORIES OF THE SAINTS

The power of the Spirit
AND THE STRONG HANDS OF FRIENDS

To bless us on life's journey
AND BRING US SAFELY HOME.
AMEN

Ruth Burgess

All Hallows

All Hallows
All Saints
All Souls
All holy.

Weekly we say the words,
'We look for the
resurrection of the dead
and the life
of the world to come.'*

Those who have died
are part of us.
We name them,
we tell their stories.

The love they had for us
and we for them
is not dead
is not forgotten.

They may be alive
in another world
but we cannot
know that.

And when we die
we do not know
what will happen
to us.

We do not know
what life there is to come.

All living
All looking
All dying
All mystery
All the journey.

Give me what I can grasp
and your love to keep me holy.
I will walk with you God.

Ruth Burgess

The Nicene Creed

Fallen leaves: a service for All Souls' (a liturgy from Dunblane Cathedral)*

Folk are given an autumn leaf as they enter the church. A table with candles and matches, enough for the entire congregation, is centrally placed.

Gathering:

We welcome you to this Service for All Souls' and hope you will find peace in this place.

All Saints' Day and All Souls' Day have been observed for most of the Church's history. On All Saints' Day we remember all those saints who left a name, whose work everyone knows something about: St Peter, St Paul, St Francis … Then on All Souls' Day we remember 'the faithful departed': the ordinary people who may not have made a mark on the world, but who made their mark on us, their loved ones.

So this is a time to remember that those who have lived were made for God and were meant for heaven. Tonight we remember them, remember that they are still part of us, and that beyond our horizons, beyond our boundaries, beyond our understanding, they are held in God's embrace.

Hymn

Prayer of approach:

We are who we are today
because of those whose lives touched ours.
God does not ask us to forget
those we have known and loved.
But sadness has to be tinged with gratitude
for lives that shaped us,
for hands that held us,
for voices that inspired us,
for love that enriched our lives.
Believing that those we remember tonight
are held in God's embrace,
we trust that we will meet them again –
in a place where there can never be farewells.
So we make our prayers
for those who now belong
to whatever it is we mean by heaven;
first our private prayers, which we make in silence,
then a spoken prayer to gather up all our thoughts.

A time of silence

Prayer:

God of all creation,
who cannot be contained by our boundaries,
by our definitions –
light from beyond the galaxies,
sea without a farther shore –
you are present in every place,
in every moment in history.
You are here and now.

Help us to know tonight
that those from whom we are separated in death –
by its long silence,
its aching absence –
are each of them in your presence;
that beyond our horizons,
beyond our boundaries,
beyond our understanding,
they are held in your embrace,
through Jesus Christ our Lord.
Amen

(Jan Sutch Pickard)

Bible reading

Hymn

Reflection

Music for meditation: (e.g. 'Intermezzo in B minor' by Brahms)

Remembering what we believe: Romans 8:31–35, 37–39

A meditation on fallen leaves:

Look at the leaf you were given when you came into the church.
At this time of the year, as the leaves fall,
we can see them in their glory better than at any other time:
just as on All Souls' Day

we can see the glory of human life all the clearer.
Look at the leaf you are holding.

It is unique.
Each has a different shape, colour, texture …
Each has its own story,
which is part of the story of creation.

Hold the leaf in the palm of your hand and touch it;
see its beauty for what it is.
Isn't its pattern remarkable?
But notice, too, that the leaf has its own rough edges.
Each one has scars, bruises and tears –
the marks of its life.
But do these marks not add to its beauty, rather than spoil it?
Once these leaves were part of a tree,
depending on it for their life.
But now, separated from the tree, does their beauty not remain?
Are they not still part of creation?
So these leaves remind us of ourselves
and also of the people who have helped to make us who we are –
those whose story we can tell,
whose pattern of life was remarkable to us,
who sometimes bore the marks and scars of life,
but whose beauty remains.
We are part of a greater life than we know,
part of God's eternal plan.
The beauty lives on,
the glory of life never fades.

The prophet Jeremiah said:
'Blessed is everyone who trusts in the Lord.
They will be like a tree planted by the waterside,
that sends out its roots along a stream.
Its leaves never fade,
it does not fail to bear fruit.'

These leaves have fulfilled their purpose,
they have done their work.

The laying of leaves and the lighting of candles:

In a moment there will be some gentle music played and you will be invited to come and
lay your leaf on the ground in front of the communion table. We will set them down so that

the leaves combine into the shape of a cross. Come in your own time, when you're ready; the music will play for as long as is needed. Place your leaf on the floor, and then go to the communion table and light a candle for someone whom you remember tonight. So we will see the cross being shaped out of the lives we remember, and we will see the lights that still shine in our lives.

Chant: ('God to enfold you', John L. Bell and Graham Maule, from *Love and Anger,* Wild Goose Publications)

Hymn

Poem:

'Tis only we who grieve

They do not leave
They are not gone
They look upon us still
They walk among the valleys now
They stride upon the hill
Their smile is in the summer sky
Their grace is in the breeze
Their memories whisper in the grass
Their calm is in the trees
Their light is in the winter snow
Their tears are in the rain
Their merriment runs in the brook
Their laughter in the lane
Their gentleness is in the flowers
They sigh in autumn leaves
They do not leave
They are not gone
'Tis only we who grieve

(Anon)

Prayers of thanksgiving:

God,
we never worship alone.
We are always surrounded by a great company
of those whose life and truth have touched our lives.
Make us aware this night
that they are with us

and we are with them.
Lord in your mercy
HEAR OUR PRAYER.

We thank you for those
who were shining lights in a dark world,
and still are:
those who in school, office, church or community
gave us the values or the faith we still live by.
Lord in your mercy
HEAR OUR PRAYER.

We thank you for the lights
that shone in just one small corner of the world:
for mothers and grandmothers,
fathers and grandfathers,
children, husbands and wives,
neighbours, friends and colleagues,
who gave us something never to be forgotten
and shared a love never to be lost.
Lord in your mercy
HEAR OUR PRAYER.

Eternal God,
you see face to face
those whom we remember here.
Tell them that we love them,
that we miss them,
that they are not forgotten.
And cheer us with the prospect of a day
when there will be no more death or parting,
and all shall be well and all shall be one.
May they whom we remember tonight
be among the first to welcome us to heaven,
where, with you in unending love,
and in the company of all the saints,
we will share the feast of your everlasting family.

Until that day,
keep us in faith, fill us with hope,
deepen us through love:
through Jesus Christ our Lord.

The Lord's Prayer

Hymn

Closing responses:

May Christ being born
anew in our hearts
bring light, healing and wholeness
to us and all our loved ones
in this world and in heaven.

AND THE SAINTS SHALL TREAD
THE PILGRIM ROAD BEFORE US,
BEHIND US,
BETWEEN US,
SURROUNDING US
WITH THE UNBOUNDED LOVE
OF GOD OUR CREATOR.

May God bless us
and heal us
and hold us in love,
today
tonight
and for evermore.
AMEN

Colin McIntosh

* Dunblane Cathedral holds this service every year. A personal invitation is sent to the relatives of those
whose funeral services have been held at the cathedral during the year.

Tell them how much we love them

These prayers were originally written for Easter Sunday, but could be used on the anniversary of a death. The setting could be a family meal, maybe between courses, with children present.

We remember today, those we love who have died:

(Those present share names, stories, photos, mementos of family members …)

We remember *(say name/s, light candle/s)* …

Tell them, God, how much we love them,
how much we miss them.
Tell them we carry their stories in our lives.

Today we rejoice that Jesus lived and died and is risen.
Today we trust you, Jesus, that there is life after death
and that you will always be with us,
loving us and leading us home.

Glory be to God,
Creator, Redeemer and Holy Spirit.
Amen

Song: (e.g. a Gloria)

or

God be with us day by day.
Jesus, join us in our play.
Holy Spirit, be our friend
now and evermore.
Amen   *(Tune: Thank you for the world so sweet)*

Ruth Burgess

Grief

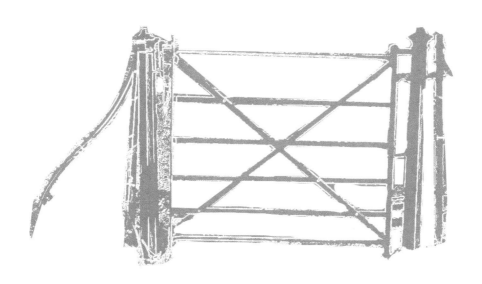

Stiff upper lip

Please, no more meaningful poems,
no cards with lilies or purple flowers on,
no uplifting verses,
no comforting bits of the Bible,
and for God's sake nothing with angels or crosses.

I'm coping really well,
so lay off with the understanding glances,
those kindly pats on the arm.
It's all over now, we get on with our lives.
She's dead, and that's that.

So perhaps I look sad sometimes – doesn't mean I can't handle it;
and someone who didn't know met me and said:
'Cheer up! You look like someone's died!'
That made me laugh, and I was glad of that,
'cause if I cry
I'll never stop.

Catherine Harkin

Loneliness

He died –
you crept in
waiting, watching
knowing that your time would come
when friends had gone and I was left alone.

They went –
you remained
gloating, grinning
knowing that I had no will
to fight you off and ban you from my home.

I bade your sister solitude to hold me in her healing gaze
but you barred the way

I searched my memory for the comfort of far better days
but I heard you say:
'That time has gone,
I am here to stay.'
You stayed
but I watched
waiting, praying
hoping that you could not freeze
each morsel of my being with your stare.

Then –
I smiled
for I knew –
praising, blessing,
loving me through all my pain
in one small corner of my heart –
God is there.

And I will let that presence grow
and force you, loneliness, to go.

Pat Welburn

Grieving for dad

I have no idea where you have gone …
well, maybe that's not totally true,
I have ideas, lots of them,
but no certainty.

You may be in another place,
another time, another reality.
You may be able to see me,
watch me growing up and old,
or you may not.

Your ashes are in your garden,
mixed with the earth.
Here, you are helping the flowers and vegetables grow,
as you did in life.

Life for you now may be going on,
you may be home,
you may be travelling,
you may be young or old.

Memories of you and mum are deep in me.
Your family, your friends,
your customers, your listeners,
still tell your story.
The memories are good.
We smile.

You had no idea where you were going,
if anywhere,
well, maybe that's not totally true either,
you were full of ideas,
you delighted in the mystery and beauty of life.

You didn't know what came next.
But you knew that God loved you,
and you knew there were no boundaries
to God's loving care.

For both of us,
that,
for now,
has to be enough.

Ruth Burgess

I wasn't really expecting God to speak to me in that church service

I wasn't really expecting God to speak to me in that church service.
I was on holiday
and went into the first church I found.
It was quite old-fashioned:
a hymn,
a prayer,
a hymn,
a children's address,
a hymn,
a Bible reading:
a hymn sandwich.
Familiar, predictable,
comfortable,
a bit twee.
I was thinking
(in a very patronising way)
Quite a nice little service,
when the minister said
that the Crucifixion was the most unfair thing
that had ever happened
in the whole of world history.

And God said:
'You've complained to me about how unfairly you've been treated.
I've told you to remember how much you have:
a loving family, many friends, a pleasant home.
We've worked through your grief on a rational level.

You understand that a completely fair world is impossible.
But I know that isn't enough.
Now you understand
that I too have been on the receiving end of unfairness.
I too have watched an innocent loved one suffer and die.
I stand with you in your grief.
I know what it is like.'

Brian Ford

Grief work

I don't know how to do this,
I don't know if it's right,
the sudden bursts of sobbing,
the dreams of you at night.

I think I see you sometimes
except I know you're dead.
Have you come back to help me?
Or am I off my head?

The books said there'd be anger,
depression, shock and rage,
but all I feel is nothing
and words blur on the page.

I carry round your photo.
I wear your silver chain.
It gives a little respite
from overwhelming pain.

I'm glad you didn't suffer,
those clichés all so true,
but nothing can make up for
the missingness of you.

Catherine Harkin

Ashes

You have kept her close
these seven years,
yet this way is one
I cannot take.

In her room
with all her fluffy toys,
photographs
and the bed in which I sleep,

is the maroon bag holding
the container with her ashes,
the cremated remains of her
in her grave-clothes.

Her release into the air of heaven,
into sea or sky, 'Who knows?',
is still constrained, held back
by your need to keep her with you.

Please, will you let her go?

Yvonne Morland

My God, my God, why?

This piece reflects the various things the bereaved have said following the three suicides that I have had to deal with over the years. Adapt as necessary.

My God, my God, why?

O God, but he was beautiful!
Such a lovely boy,
cheeky, full of fun,
the life and soul of the party.
Such a caring boy,
looking out for his brothers and sisters –
he'd do anything to help anyone.
My beautiful, beautiful boy!

My God, my God, why?

Why did he leave us?
He had so much to live for –
partner, children, career.
Why didn't he confide in us?
We could have helped:
a problem shared is a problem solved.

My God, my God, why?

Why did he forsake us?
Was he just so wrapped up
in a despair we never saw was there?
Why did he make that awful choice?
Did he see no other solution,
or did some switch in his brain simply flip,
like the psychologist said?

My God, my God, why?

Did he know he would leave us with this guilt,
this pain,
this confusion,
this despair,
this anger,
this grief?
So many questions,
and I don't understand.
I just don't understand!
Do you understand, God?

My God, my God, why?

David Hamflett

Grief (for my sister Agnes)

I do not feel your presence near
like some comforting wraith.
Only a dullness and a heavy weight of gloom.

In your dying, hard as it was to watch –
you struggled for breath and sipped water through a straw –
there was a calmness born of necessity,
a gentleness to our exchanges.

Your children held your hand.
And, when awake, you acknowledged us all
with customary wry humour.
'I see you're not wearing black yet.'

In the relatives' room we drank tea
and joked and laughed
to counter feelings too deep to share.
In the end you slipped away quietly.

At the funeral the priest admitted
to sharing your love of musicals
and even crooned some Doris Day,
as we smiled indulgently.

We did what we had to do.

The hugs, the cards, the flowers
and the sometimes clumsy touches of acquaintances
moved me with their vulnerability and shy beauty.

It was later, alone, I opened my Christmas present
you'd wrapped and labelled before your heart attack:
an angel figurine, complete with harp.

Mary Hanrahan

Bye love (for Enid)

Bye love
that's what you said to me
every Boxing Day,
after the rugby
and the sausage pies.

Bye love
that's what you always said to me
as a child and an adult,
when we said goodbye.

Bye love
that's what you said to me
when I last saw you
in hospital care.

Bye love
the words and the loving
far deeper in you
than dementia could go.

Bye love
it's me now that says it.

Bye love
and God bless you
as you journey safe home.

Ruth Burgess

You are near (for Dorothy)

You were the only self-proclaimed atheist
in our family,
and you were my godmother.
God, I suspect, did not object.

When you died
I took from your house
a ship's wheel

a polished table
a lethal wartime tin-opener
a spade that had survived a shed full of woodworm
and some tiny plastic Christmas trees
I'd always loved.

There is not time to tell
of the drawers full of linen
and cupboards of china
and the fur coats
and the bills to tell us what they cost you
and the button box
and the sword.
There is not time …
but they were all there.

I do not grieve for you
you were too alive
too full of laughter and stories and mischief
for me to be sad.

You are near
when I weave red tinsel
round the ship's wheel each Advent,
blow dust from your table,
dig deep into soil.

You gave me love and the courage to be different.
I am grateful.

I think you will forgive me
when with a smile
I bring you into my prayers.

Ruth Burgess

No trite words

No trite words of benediction take away the pain.
No soft words of resurrection bring him back again.
Here beyond your words of comfort, lonely, lost I sit.
While you scatter pearls of wisdom, I just feel the grit.
While you talk about your children, watch them come and go,
I will tend a tiny grave and watch the flowers grow.

Andrew Pratt

A liturgy on a hospital ward

Adapted from a liturgy done on a ward, at the staff's request, following a difficult time.

Welcome

Opening sentences:

Our God is a God
who longs to be with us:
in our deepest places,
in our sadness and tears.

Our God is a God
who holds us compassionately:
bringing us comfort,
sharing our pain.

Our God is like a rock:
unmoved from love,
firm beneath our feet.

Readings

Action:

A large candle is lit to symbolise the lives of the patients on the ward. Each person may come and light their own small candle and share something they remember about a patient who was significant for them.

Silence or music

Closing prayers:

We place in the hands of God
all that disturbs us,
all that causes us pain.

We place into the hollow of God's hands
all the patients past and present
and everything that they meant or mean to us.

We place into the loving hands of God
all who have gone before us for whom we still mourn.

God is our refuge.
Underneath us, always,
are God's everlasting arms. *(Deut 33:27)*
Amen

Blessing and dismissal:

And now let us go into the world,
and may God be our company:
Christ Jesus who walks before us
and the Spirit who surrounds us with a cloud of grace.
God's blessing be upon us and those we love,
this day and evermore.
Amen

Kes Grant

Emptiness

Dear God,
this is one of those days when everything around me
brings a stark reminder of my loss.
The book with paper marking the place
beyond which nothing will ever be read.
That favourite mug, unused now,
but never to be discarded.
The biscuits I don't eat but bought for you.
It's so often the smallest reminders that bring the sudden tears.
I wept when I found that unwashed handkerchief
in a pocket of clothes for the charity shop.
I was overwhelmed
when I found the birthday card,
signed and sealed and ready for my special day.
And when I look over to that chair …

All those empty spaces.
All those unfinished, everyday things.
Oh God! I wish! I wish …

Caring God,
people tell me that the hurt will fade with time,
but that's not how I feel today.
Today is bleak and lonely.
Hold out your arms of love to me,
especially at those times when I feel that you're not there.
Touch me with your care
and help me to recognise when someone else is doing that
on your behalf.
I need you. Now!

Marjorie Dobson

Grief is a thief

Grief is a thief,
a mugger.
There you are strolling along
quite joco –
then that sickening whack of the cosh
sending you sprawling
at the sight of a certain walk
a tone of voice –
it's him!

Oh no, it's not. He's dead.
And down you go, face smashed against the ground
as grief-thief rolls you over
and steals another memory.

Catherine Harkin

Left

There are times when I am so angry with him.
How could he have done such a thing to me? Such a selfish thing!
He's now out of the picture. All his problems are solved.
He couldn't cope with life, so he ended it all.
Finished! Done! Let somebody else clear up the mess.
And that means me.
Didn't he recognise that the shock of finding him could have killed me?
Or was he so wrapped up in his own misery that he didn't even consider that?
Oh God. Why?
Why did he not talk about his despair?
Why didn't he trust me enough to try to explain?
How can I live with this guilt?
Should I have noticed something?
Will I ever forgive myself?
Or him?
Will I ever get over this?
God, if you're there and if you care,
please listen and understand.
I need someone who can.

Marjorie Dobson

My being yearns for Easter

My being yearns for Easter.
New life bursting from cracked and broken earth.
I scarcely dare believe that
this besmirched greyness,
this constricting,
constrictive bulb of pain within
may sprout
a daffodil.

Mary Hanrahan

Life goes on

I was sitting alone in a local restaurant eating dinner when a beautiful older woman came in and requested a table for five. She sat down, and a few minutes later her husband joined her, carrying a seasonal bouquet of flowers. The two of them sat quietly together for about a half an hour, before the woman set a framed black-and-white photograph of a young girl beside the flowers on the table.

I smiled over, and the woman explained that the girl was their daughter, and that it was the one-year anniversary of her death. She went on to say that they were waiting for their other daughter and her two children to arrive: this restaurant was the last place that they were all together before her daughter had suddenly died.

I couldn't help but watch as this family tearfully celebrated her life and shared all that they miss in their relationship with her, while the girl's niece and nephew drew pictures and giggled, as only children can.

I was moved by the family's ritual to mark the one-year anniversary – and can think of no more beautiful way to mark a milestone like this than to sit around a table with family – complete with pictures, crayons and mimosas.

Thanks be to God for all the rituals
we create to remember loved ones
and to remind ourselves that life
indeed
does go on ...

A. A. Masters

Life goes on – words for the journey

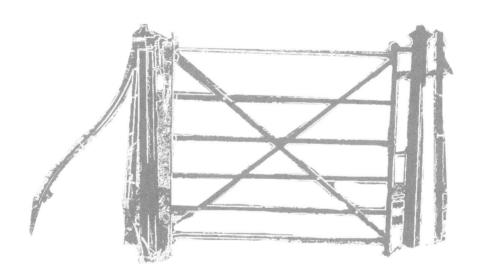

All the nights and days

The blessing of God our maker be ours,
hope and courage,
and strength and healing,
all the nights and days
of our journey home.

Ruth Burgess

Dark clouds and sunlight

May the God
who dances
in the dark clouds
and the sunlight
keep you
and cherish you
in loving kindness
and hope.

Ruth Burgess

A journey with angels and friends

May the blessing of God surround us.
May angels and friends share our journey.
May we be wise and strong and creative.
May we celebrate beauty and love.

May God's image grow within us.
May laughter and wonder heal us.
May the gospel of life sustain us.
All the days of our journey home.

Ruth Burgess

Blessing and wonder

The blessing of tears and laughter be ours.
The company of friends and family be ours.
The hope of budding trees and sunlight be ours.
The wonder of the twinkling stars be ours.
The promise of sunrise and healing be ours.
Ours today and every day.

Let us go now, into life and love.

Ruth Burgess

Beckon us God

Beckon us God,
with your smile of welcome,
with your sure, strong calling,
beckon us in the morning.

Challenge us God,
with your love and justice,
with your truth and travelling,
challenge us in the noontide.

Keep us God,
with your saints and angels,
with your friends and little ones,
keep us in the evening.

Cradle us God,
with your songs and stories,
with your hope and healing,
cradle us till dawning.

Ruth Burgess

The blessing of the common life

Warm and strong,
green and growing,
the blessing of the earth be ours.

Wide and free,
with the wind whistling,
the blessing of the heavens be ours.

Today and tomorrow,
the seasons turning,
the blessing of the years be ours.

Memories and stories
and a million questions,
the blessing of eternity be ours.

We are so small
but we are loved and cherished,
the blessing of the common life be ours.

Ours today and in the days to come.

Ruth Burgess

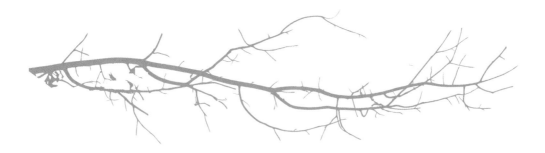

For ever and ever

The blessing of the Maker of all
the healing of the Storyteller
the comfort and cheer of the breath of life
be ours for ever and ever.

Ruth Burgess

We arise and go forth

We arise and go forth on the journey before us,
knowing that where Christ leads,
life is a journey home.
Therefore we travel in faith, in hope and in love.

In the name and in the blessing of God,
Father, Son and Holy Spirit.
Amen

Ian Cowie

God our maker, our mother, our friend

May God our maker, our mother, our friend
wrap us in wholeness,
keep us in kindness
and bless our journey homewards.
Amen

Frances Blodwell, née Copsey

Life without end

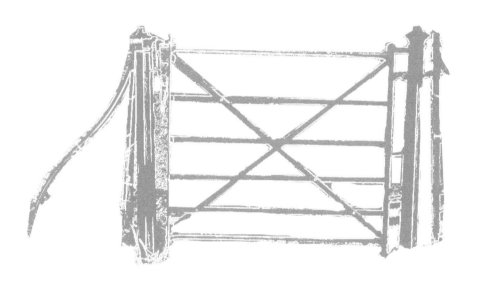

We are wonderfully made (Ps 139:14)

We are made up
of stardust and stories
of warmth and wonder
of blood and bread.

We are made up
of seeds and sinews
of hope and harvest
of living and dead.

We are made up
of genes and memories
of tears and laughter
of bones and breath.

We are made up
of God and glory
of love and questions
of life and death.

Ruth Burgess

Step by step

Step by step
in your footprints
Brendan, Brigit,
Columba, Adamnan.

Step by step
in your footprints
Margaret, Cormac
Anna, Michael.

Step by step
in your footprints
Sue, Kate,
Ian, Alice.

Step by step
in your footprints,
all you saints,
all you angels,
step by step,
I'm coming home.

Ruth Burgess

Today and every day

The blessing of the turning tides
The blessing of the young crow calling
The blessing of the sun and moon
The blessing of the early morning
The blessing of the autumn leaves
The blessing of the pilgrim way
The blessing of love and life and death
Be ours today and every day.

Ruth Burgess

Credo

In life.
In death.
God loves us.

In life.
In death.
God cares what happens to us.

In life.
In death.
God asks us to be loving.

In life.
In death.
God does not abandon us.

In life.
In death.
God loves us.

Life without end?

Amen

Ruth Burgess

Appendix

Planning a funeral order

For professionals

If you are a professional leading a funeral service encourage family members and friends to share in the planning.

- Explain the structure of the service to them (you may choose to depart from this structure).

- Listen to any ideas they have about what they want to include in the service.

- Find out if the person who has died has expressed any preference for actions or readings or music.

- If the person who has died was creative, or had a particular strong interest in something, do you want to include indications of this in the funeral? Hangings on the wall … music or stories they have written … a golf club, knitting needles, vegetables, a scrabble board on or near the coffin? …

- Provide family members/friends with resource books or websites if they need to choose readings or music.

- Build up a few copies of a loose leaf folder of sacred and secular readings, songs and prayers that you can leave with family and friends for them to look at.

- Provide them with examples of appropriate participative activities: lighting candles, releasing balloons …

- Ask if any of them would like to give a tribute during the service, and support them in doing this … Help them, if necessary, to craft it, and offer to read it before the funeral. The tribute can include pictures, music and song …

- If possible, visit the place where the funeral is to take place and rehearse any involvement. This is particularly important if children are taking part in the funeral. If this is not possible, look at photos of the inside of the building whilst planning the funeral.

- Work with family and friends to create a printed order of service. Give them examples of what is possible.

- Ask if there are local, religious or family customs that they would like to observe, e.g. bringing the coffin into the church the night before the funeral, carrying the coffin into the church or crematorium …

- Do they want a Book of Remembrance available for people to sign and to record memories at the funeral and/or later at a funeral meal?

- Try to visit family/friends at least twice in order to give people time and space to think about and discuss with others the shape of the funeral and its contents. If this is not possible, provide contact details so that they can talk to you and let you know their ideas and choices.

- Be aware of time constraints when planning the service, especially when including participative activities. They can take longer than you think.

For family and friends

If you have never planned a funeral before, but want to, there are plenty of resources to help you do this. Talking with clergy and leaders of secular funeral services may be helpful. Undertakers vary, but many can be knowledgeable in pointing to what is possible in your local area and in accessing resources. A list of helpful websites and books is given at the back of this book.

Where, what and when

The traditional pattern for a funeral is a funeral service in church followed by a burial or cremation. More recent developments include a private cremation or burial followed by a thanksgiving service, or for the whole funeral to take place either in a crematorium or at the graveside. The scattering or burial of ashes can occur at any time after a cremation and can be a private or public occasion. A private cremation followed by a public thanksgiving and scattering or burial of ashes is also a possibility. Often a meal is held after the funeral to allow people to share memories and support each other.

In church

If the funeral is to be held in a church, the church may have a set order of service that cannot be fundamentally changed, but can be personalised by the choice of readings and by actions and by the telling of the person's story. Services in churches are usually led by local clergy.

In other places

If the funeral is to be held in a crematorium, or in a private house, or in the open air, there are few restrictions on the funeral order or on who leads the funeral ceremony.

Structures of funeral orders

The structure of a Christian funeral follows the same basic pattern as other acts of Christian worship:

- an approach to God
- a listening to God's Word
- a response to the Word
- a sending out into the world

Within the approach to God there should be a welcoming of people to the funeral. God's Word can include non-biblical readings.

Within the response to the Word there is usually a telling of the person's story, a prayer for mourners, a commending (entrusting) of the person to God, and a committal (a leaving of the person with God).

The sending out into the world includes a blessing for those present.

In a secular funeral the pattern will usually include:

- a welcoming

- some thoughts/readings on life and death

- a telling of the person's story

- saying goodbye/a committal

- closing words/support for those who mourn

Some notes on the funeral order

- Ensure that the funeral order has structure: a beginning, a middle and an end.

- Choose readings, music and actions that fit into the structure.

- Choose short readings that can be understood on the first reading.

- If there are children present include readings or songs or actions that they can participate in and understand.

- Include some silence and/or music to allow people space for their own thoughts and prayers.

- If you are including participative songs try to ascertain if they will be familiar to those present and arrange musical accompaniment.

- A printed order of service can include photos and readings. (Most funeral directors will be able to arrange this, or you can produce your own.)

- If there are any responsive readings indicate this clearly on the order of service.

General notes

- The leadership of the funeral can be shared.

- It is helpful for one person to have an overall knowledge of the funeral order so that, if necessary, they can assist or take over from a participant on the day.

- When using symbolic actions, e.g. lighting candles, ensure everyone can see what is happening.

- Symbolic actions take time; allow for this in the funeral planning.

- If you want people to bring things to the funeral, e.g. individual flowers or petals to place on the coffin, they need to be aware of this. Include it in the funeral notice before the funeral. Similarly, if you want family to fill in the grave you may need to provide shovels.

In a crematorium

- Crematoriums usually allot a fixed time to funerals. If you think the funeral you are planning will take longer it is usually possible to book a double slot.

- You may want to decorate the funeral space, ask for some items in the crematorium to be removed or covered, or to rearrange chairs. If what you want to do will take time, it is usually better to book a slot at the beginning or end of a day.

- There are usually limitations as to what can be placed inside a coffin.

At the graveside

- In some communities there is a tradition of family members and friends carrying the coffin and lowering the coffin into the grave.

- If you want family members to fill in the grave, you need to arrange this with your undertaker.

- Words at the graveside usually consist of a brief committal and blessing, if the main funeral service has taken place elsewhere.

- If you are using an order of service remember that it may rain! Have a waterproof folder at hand, and give people clear instructions if there are responses.

Ashes

There are very few restrictions in Britain regarding where ashes can be scattered or buried. The decision about what to do with a person's ashes is usually taken by the same people who organised the funeral. The person who has died may have formally or informally left instructions as to what to do. Words to accompany the scattering or burying of ashes are included in this book, as are relevant websites.

Ruth Burgess

Some ideas for a day conference on funerals

In the publicity make it clear that the day is open both to professionals and to anyone who wants to talk about funerals and explore available resources.

Displays

- Resources relating to the different types of coffins and shrouds available. If possible, have some coffins and shrouds on display, e.g. wicker, cardboard, pictorial, wool, etc.

- Examples of printed orders of funeral services.

- Books relating to funeral services and practicalities.

- A list of relevant websites, with a computer available to explore websites.

- Storybooks and workbooks for children relating to death and funerals.

- Memorial stones, benches, books, etc.

- A wall covered with paper for participants to add details of resources they have found useful.

Workshops

- Invite local undertakers to run an 'Any Questions' session relating to local crematoria, church facilities and burial facilities. Explore what is and what isn't possible locally.

- A workshop open to all who conduct funerals, particularly exploring good practice in involving families in putting together funeral liturgies and making funeral arrangements.

- Children attending funerals. What can we do to make funerals child- and family-friendly?

- How do you put a funeral liturgy together? A look at songs, prayers, participative actions, readings.

- How do I arrange a funeral? What needs to be done? Who do I talk to? A look at the legal side and the practicalities.

- What kind of funeral do I want? Who do I need to tell? How can I tell them? What is it useful for people to know? A look at what you can do to help others to carry out your wishes.

- Funerals without God. What resources are available? Who could I ask locally to lead a non-religious funeral?

- What can we do with the ashes? A discussion on practicalities, possibilities, good practice and resources.

- Co-creating funerals: an opportunity for professionals and lay people to work together to create one or two funeral liturgies, based on case histories or examples drawn from the group.

- An opportunity to remember and grieve and celebrate. What kind of liturgies are held locally to enable the grieving process? What kind of rituals and liturgies would people welcome? Good practice from elsewhere.

General

- Have an artist in residence painting a coffin. (A coffin for an individual present at the conference? A coffin of the artist's choice?) Ask the artist to bring in a range of designs.

- You may wish to ask a group that caters for funerals to provide lunch/refreshments on the day.

- If you are holding the day conference in a church setting you may wish to offer a participative liturgy, relating to life, death and bereavement, during the day.

- Take names of those interested and arrange a later visit to local undertakers' premises, crematoria and burial places.

Helpful websites and books

These books are from many different publishers. More information can be found on the Internet.

Stories for younger children about death and grieving

Water Bugs and Dragonflies, Doris Stickney
Badger's Parting Gifts, Susan Varley
Always and Forever, Alan Durant
Grandad's Prayers of the Earth, Douglas Wood
Granpa, John Burningham
Muddles, Puddles and Sunshine, Diana Crossley (workbook)
Help Me Say Goodbye, Janis Silverman (workbook)
The Best Day of the Week, Hannah Cole
Grandad's Ashes, Walter Smith
Talking with Children and Young People about Death and Dying, Mary Turner (workbook)
I Miss You, Pat Thomas

Stories for older children

Mama's Going to Buy You a Mockingbird, Jean Little
See Ya, Simon, David Hill
A Taste of Blackberries, Doris Buchanan Smith
Two Weeks with the Queen, Morris Gleitzman

Websites and articles: children and grief

Winston's Wish: www.winstonswish.org.uk
Childline: www.childline.org.uk
Childhood Bereavement Network: www.childhoodbereavementnetwork.org.uk
Bereavement Advice Centre: downloadable booklet *My Grandad Plants People!*:
www.bereavementadvice.org/uploads/DOC493E84D9E7709.pdf
Grief Encounter: www.griefencounter.org.uk
Macmillan: www.macmillan.org.uk
Marie Curie: www.mariecurie.org.uk
The Compassionate Friends UK: www.tcf.org.uk
'I had no chance to say goodbye', Kate Hilpern, article in *The Guardian* 13/7/13

General books

The Dead Good Funerals Book, Sue Gill and John Fox
Meaningful Funerals: Meeting the Theological and Pastoral Challenge in a Postmodern Era,
Ewan Kelly
All in the End Is Harvest, Agnes Whitaker

Poems and Readings for Funerals, Julia Watson
Loss: An Anthology, Elspeth Barker (Ed.)
Funerals without God, Jane Wynne Willson
Funerals, James Bentley, Andrew Best, Jackie Hunt

General websites

www.scattering-ashes.co.uk
www.co-operativefuneralcare
www.naturalendings.co.uk
www.funeralhelper.org
http://belfast.humanists.net/FUNERAL%20POETRY.htm
www.sayinggoodbye.org
www.goodlifedeathgrief.org.uk
http://dyingmatters.org

Space for other ideas and readings

Space for other ideas and readings

Space for other ideas and readings

Space for other ideas and readings

Space for other ideas and readings

Space for other ideas and readings

Sources and acknowledgements

'Special pleading' – by Kate McIlhagga, from *The Green Heart of the Snowdrop*, Kate McIlhagga, Wild Goose Publications, 2004

'The time that's left' – by Kate McIlhagga, from *The Green Heart of the Snowdrop*, Kate McIlhagga, Wild Goose Publications, 2004

'A prayer for Peggy' – by Ruth Burgess, from *Friends and Enemies: A Book of Short Prayers and Some Ways to Write Your Own*, Ruth Burgess, Wild Goose Publications, 2004

'For my mother' – by Jan Sutch Pickard, from *The Pattern of Our Days: Liturgies and Resources for Worship,* Kathy Galloway (Ed.), Wild Goose Publications, 1999

'Dancing in the streets' – by Ian M. Fraser, from *Friends and Enemies: A Book of Short Prayers and Some Ways to Write Your Own*, Ruth Burgess, Wild Goose Publications, 2004

'Sealing a coffin' – by Kate McIlhagga, from *Candles and Conifers: Resources for All Saints' and Advent*, Ruth Burgess (Ed.), Wild Goose Publications, 2005

'Liturgy for a stillborn child' – by Kate McIlhagga, from *The Pattern of Our Days: Liturgies and Resources for Worship,* Kathy Galloway (Ed.), Wild Goose Publications, 1999

'Remember' – by Andrew Pratt, from *Poppies and Snowdrops: Resources for Times of Grief and Bereavement,* Andrew Pratt and Majorie Dobson, Inspire (Methodist Publishing House)

'A simple funeral liturgy' – originally published in *The Glory of Blood, Sweat and Tears: Liturgies for Living and Dying*, Dorothy McRae-McMahon, Uniting Church Publishing House, 1996 (out of print) © Dorothy McRae-McMahon. Used by permission of Dorothy McRae-McMahon

'An order of service for a funeral' – by Andrew Pratt, from *Poppies and Snowdrops: Resources for Times of Grief and Bereavement,* Andrew Pratt and Majorie Dobson, Inspire (Methodist Publishing House)

'Over' – by Ruth Burgess, from *At Ground Level*, Ruth Burgess, Wild Goose Publications (out of print)

'Remember' – by Debra Mullaly, from *Candles and Conifers: Resources for All Saints' and Advent*, Ruth Burgess (Ed.), Wild Goose Publications, 2005

'A conversation' – by Ruth Burgess, from *Pushing the Boat Out: New Poetry*, Kathy Galloway (Ed.), Wild Goose Publications, 1995

'This is the place', by Marjorie Dobson, from *Multi-coloured Maze*, Marjorie Dobson, Stainer and Bell 2004. Used by permission of Marjorie Dobson and Stainer and Bell.

'Responses for a burial' – by Ruth Burgess, from *The Pattern of Our Days: Liturgies and Resources for Worship,* Kathy Galloway (Ed.), Wild Goose Publications, 1999

'Responses for a cremation' – by Ruth Burgess, from *The Pattern of Our Days: Liturgies and Resources for Worship,* Kathy Galloway (Ed.), Wild Goose Publications, 1999

'The communion of saints' – by Kathy Galloway, from *Talking to the Bones*, Kathy Galloway, SPCK, 1996. © Kathy Galloway. Used by permission of Kathy Galloway.

'Snowdrops' – by Simon Taylor. This piece originally appeared as a Saturday sermon in the *Plymouth Evening Herald* in March 1998. Used by permission of Simon Taylor.

'Memorial' – by Marjorie Dobson, from *Poppies and Snowdrops: Resources for Times of Grief and Bereavement,* Andrew Pratt and Majorie Dobson, Inspire (Methodist Publishing House)

'I didn't go to her grave today' – by Marjorie Dobson, from *Poppies and Snowdrops: Resources for Times of Grief and Bereavement,* Andrew Pratt and Majorie Dobson, Inspire (Methodist Publishing House)

'Liturgy for the anniversary of a death' – by Ruth Burgess, from *The Pattern of Our Days: Liturgies and Resources for Worship,* Kathy Galloway (Ed.), Wild Goose Publications, 1999. Also published in *A Book of a Thousand Prayers*, Angela Ashwin, Zondervan, 2002. Used by permission of Ruth Burgess © Ruth Burgess

'All Hallows' – by Ruth Burgess, from *Acorns and Archangels: Resources for Ordinary Time – the Feast of the Transfiguration to All Hallows',* Ruth Burgess (Ed.), Wild Goose Publications, 2009

'God of all creation, who cannot be contained by our boundaries' prayer – by Jan Sutch Pickard, from *Candles and Conifers: Resources for All Saints' and Advent*, Ruth Burgess (Ed.), Wild Goose Publications, 2005

'Tell them how much we love them' – by Ruth Burgess, from *Eggs and Ashes: Practical and Liturgical Resources for Lent and Holy Week,* by Ruth Burgess and Chris Polhill (Eds), Wild Goose Publication, 2007

'Loneliness' – by Pat Welburn, from *Praying for the Dawn: A Resource Book for the Ministry of Healing*, by Ruth Burgess and Kathy Galloway (Eds), Wild Goose Publications, 2000

'No trite words' – by Andrew Pratt, from *Poppies and Snowdrops: Resources for Times of Grief and Bereavement,* Andrew Pratt and Majorie Dobson, Inspire (Methodist Publishing House)

'Emptiness' – by Marjorie Dobson, from *Poppies and Snowdrops: Resources for Times of Grief and Bereavement,* Andrew Pratt and Majorie Dobson, Inspire (Methodist Publishing House)

'Left' – by Marjorie Dobson, from *Poppies and Snowdrops: Resources for Times of Grief and Bereavement,* Andrew Pratt and Majorie Dobson, Inspire (Methodist Publishing House)

'We rise and go forth' – by Ian Cowie, from *A Book of Blessings and How to Write Your Own*, Ruth Burgess (ed.), Wild Goose Publications, 2001

'God our maker, our mother, our friend' – by Frances Copsey, from *A Book of Blessings and How to Write Your Own*, Ruth Burgess (ed.), Wild Goose Publications, 2001

About the authors

Jan Berry is a minister within the United Reformed Church working in theological education at Luther King House, Manchester. She enjoys creating liturgies and material for worship, and has had several pieces published in Wild Goose anthologies, as well as producing her own collection, *Naming God* (Granary Press).

Lindsay Louise Biddle is a writer and Presbyterian Church (USA) minister who lives in Glasgow and serves as chaplain of Affirmation Scotland and as a minister locum for the Church of Scotland.

Frances Blodwell, née Copsey – Throughout her life Frances cared passionately about women's issues. When she had to endure the loss of children in a series of miscarriages she was able to allay the desperation of this experience to some extent by addressing its glaring neglect in the liturgy of the Church. At the time, no one else seemed to be doing so. Later she developed an unremitting and eventually totally disabling form of MS. Whilst still able she expressed this devastation in poems of searing honesty. The illness took away her power of speech but could not touch her generous and loving spirit.

Irene Bruce – After retirement from welfare work Irene remained busy with volunteering and family caring. She is now slowing down, and enjoys seeing friends and family.

Nick Burden is an associate of the Iona Community. He worships at St Gabriel's Church, Heaton.

Ruth Burgess is a member of the Iona Community. She is busy being retired, writing, watching the antics of crows and jackdaws and growing vegetables. Ruth lives in Dunblane

John Butterfield is a minister working in Central Scotland and a member of the Iona Community. He is married to Caroline and they have two grown-up children.

Ian Cowie (1923-2005) was a minister in the Church of Scotland and one of the early members of the Iona Community. He was deeply involved in the healing ministry, and his books about it still reach a wide audience.

Roddy Cowie is a professor of psychology, a Lay Reader in the Church of Ireland, and an associate member of the Iona Community, with links to the Abbey and Iona going back to his childhood.

James Curry is an associate member of the Iona Community. Having spent the last seven and a half years in the Highlands of Scotland, he is now Priest-in-Charge of two churches near Huddersfield.

Judy Dinnen is a parish priest, hospital chaplain and associate member of the Iona Community. She responds to faith, life's joys and sorrows with her pen or keypad. The reflection in this book was written to a special cousin, who was a music therapist.

Carol Dixon was born in Alnwick, Northumberland and is a lay preacher in the United Reformed Church. Her hymns and prayers have been published in *All Year Round*, *Songs for the New Millennium*, *Worship Live*, the Church of Scotland hymnbook and on HymnQuest. She is a wife, mother and grandmother. Her twin sons, Simon and Colin Dixon, have collaborated with her in some of her writing.

Marjorie Dobson is a Methodist Local Preacher and writer of hymns, prayers, poetry and drama for worship. She had a solo collection of work published in 2004 and has co-authored two further collections with Andrew Pratt, published in 2006 and 2008.

Brian Ford: I was a biology teacher for the whole of my paid working life. I retired six years ago and almost exactly twelve months later my wife died from cancer.

Sally Foster-Fulton is the associate minister at Dunblane Cathedral and the Convener of the Church of Scotland's Church and Society Council. Sally is originally from South Carolina, is married to Stuart; they have two beautifully creative and unique daughters, Alex and Gracie.

Ian M. Fraser is one of the original members of the Iona Community. He is 95 years old.

Kathy Galloway is a member of the Iona Community, and a writer, theologian and activist. She is the Head of Christian Aid Scotland and lives in Glasgow.

Kes Grant: I am an unorthodox Church of England priest. Previously I was a hospital chaplain and now work as a full-time school chaplain.

Christine Green is a member of the Iona Community living in Cumbria. She is a legal secretary, and a voluntary befriender with SANDS (Stillbirth And Neonatal Death Society).

Liz Gregory-Smith lives on the edge of Durham City with her husband, David. Liz is an Anglican Reader with permission to officiate in the local Anglican church.

David Hamflett is a Methodist minister and a Friend of the Iona Community working in the north of England, and has a special interest in compiling and composing liturgies. He sings traditional folk songs and plays the guitar and the bodhrán and has just taken up the Irish bouzouki.

Mary Hanrahan: I am currently enjoying my retirement, learning new skills in craft and writing groups and rediscovering wonder by spending time with my grandson, Tom. I am an active member in my parish community of St Paul the Apostle, Shettleston and a regular poet at Lentfest, our Archdiocesan celebration of the arts.

Catherine Harkin is a member of the Iona Community who lives and works in Edinburgh as a GP, writer, singer and many other identities.

John Harvey is a retired Church of Scotland parish minister, and a member of the Iona Community. With his wife, Molly, he has been involved recently in supporting the work of the Poverty Truth Commission in Glasgow and west central Scotland.

Anne Lawson is Vicar of Haslington and Crewe Green and Chaplain to the Cheshire Agricultural Society.

Ashley-Anne Masters is ordained in the Presbyterian Church (USA) and is a pastor, author and hospital chaplain in Chicago, IL. She is author of *Holding Hope: Grieving Pregnancy Loss During Advent* (Church Health Center) and co-author of *Bless Her Heart: Life as a Young Clergywoman* (Chalice Press). She blogs at revaam.org.

Joy Mead is a member of the Iona Community and the author of several Wild Goose books.

Kate McIlhagga was a minister and a member of the Iona Community until her death in 2002. Her intimate, insightful prayers and poems are loved and used by people far and wide for both personal and group prayer and reflection.

Colin McIntosh recently retired after 25 years as minister of Dunblane Cathedral. Previously he was minster of St John's-Renfield Church in Glasgow.

Dorothy McRae-McMahon is a minister in the Uniting Church in Australia. She is the author of several books, including *Liturgies for the Journey of Life* and *Liturgies for Daily Life* (SPCK).

Yvonne Morland has been a member of the Iona Community since 2002 and has contributed to many other Wild Goose anthologies.

Andrew Pratt is a Methodist minister and hymn writer who has taught Pastoral and Practical Theology to people preparing for ministry at Luther King House in Manchester.

Katherine Rennie is a member of the Iona Community and a local preacher with the Methodist Church.

Ken Russell has served as a parish minister and a hospital chaplain. He now serves as a prison chaplain.

Norman Shanks is a member of the Iona Community, a retired Church of Scotland minister, and a non-executive director of NHS Greater Glasgow and Clyde.

Marilyn Shedden lives happily with her partner, Maggie, their dogs and other animals in a beautiful part of Kintyre, where she enjoys golf and photography.

Jan Sutch Pickard is a poet and storyteller living on the Isle of Mull. She is a member of the Iona Community, a former Warden of Iona Abbey and a former Ecumenical Accompanier, who is now involved, through volunteering and leading worship, in her local community.

Simon Taylor is a Baptist minister and university chaplain in Exeter.

Zam Walker is a minister of the United Reformed Church in Greenock who job-shares ministry and childcare with her husband, David Coleman. Both are members of the Iona Community.

Ewing Wallace is the church secretary of Dunblane Cathedral and a member of the cathedral choir. He enjoys hill walking and photography.

Pat Welburn is a member of the Iona Community, a retired guardian *ad litem*, a mother, grandmother and great-grandmother.

Wellspring is the name used by Catherine McElhinney and Kathryn Turner for their worship and spirituality resources. Catherine is a primary teacher in the south of England; Kathryn heads up the Spirituality Department in the Diocese of Hexham and Newcastle. Their website is used by people around the world: www.wellsprings.org.uk

Index of authors

Andrew Pratt 74, 97-99, 182
Katherine Rennie 21, 35, 160
Ken Russell 59

Norman Shanks 83-84, 85-86,
Marilyn Shedden 30-31
Jan Sutch Pickard 34, 87-89, 144

Simon Taylor 149

Zam Walker 26, 78-81
Pat Welburn 173
Wellspring 45-47

Wild Goose Publications is part of the Iona Community:

- An ecumenical movement of men and women from different walks of life and different traditions in the Christian church
- Committed to the gospel of Jesus Christ, and to following where that leads, even into the unknown
- Engaged together, and with people of goodwill across the world, in acting, reflecting and praying for justice, peace and the integrity of creation
- Convinced that the inclusive community we seek must be embodied in the community we practise

Together with our staff, we are responsible for:

- Our islands residential centres of Iona Abbey, the MacLeod Centre on Iona, and Camas Adventure Centre on the Ross of Mull

and in Glasgow:

- The administration of the Community
- Our work with young people
- Our publishing house, Wild Goose Publications
- Our association in the revitalising of worship with the Wild Goose Resource Group

The Iona Community was founded in Glasgow in 1938 by George MacLeod, minister, visionary and prophetic witness for peace, in the context of the poverty and despair of the Depression. Its original task of rebuilding the monastic ruins of Iona Abbey became a sign of hopeful rebuilding of community in Scotland and beyond. Today, we are about 250 Members, mostly in Britain, and 1500 Associate Members, with 1400 Friends worldwide. Together and apart, 'we follow the light we have, and pray for more light'.

For information on the Iona Community contact:
The Iona Community, Fourth Floor, Savoy House, 140 Sauchiehall Street,
Glasgow G2 3DH, UK. Phone: 0141 332 6343
e-mail: admin@iona.org.uk; web: www.iona.org.uk

For enquiries about visiting Iona, please contact:
Iona Abbey, Isle of Iona, Argyll PA76 6SN, UK. Phone: 01681 700404
e-mail: ionacomm@iona.org.uk